Pathway to peace

A MEMOIR

JOCELYN HALL

Pathway to Peace, A Memoir

Copyright © 2023 by Jocelyn Hall

All rights reserved. This book or any portion thereof may not be reproduced or used in any manner whatsoever without the express written permission of the publisher except for the use of brief quotations in a book review.

Printed in the United States of America
First Print 2023

ISBN: 979-8-9879471-0-4 Print
ISBN: 979-8-9879471-1-1 E-book

DEDICATION

To the only wise God who thought so much of me that He entrusted me with this memoir, I cannot begin to say thank you for getting me through so much in this life. When I had moments of giving up, your Spirit refreshed me. I do not know why you chose me, but I am eternally grateful.

To my parents Joseph and Dorothy Hall, I am so blessed to have you both in my life. Even in the years of grace, you still are my encouragement. I hope that I have made you proud as a daughter and mother. Love ya, love ya, love ya!

To my brother Joseph Hall Jr, you are the best cheerleader in my life and my Peter! I hope you know without doubt that I love you beyond our years. You were the first in all things with me, and of course I will proclaim this to the world. My Twin and baby brother, thank you.

To my DeMaris, the unsung hero: I can't begin to express how much I love you. You have been my backbone and exemplified strength that only God could have given you. This ride we went on was crazy, but we made it! I know Cameron is so proud of the man you've become. Don't change! Be yourself and soar.

To Terry and the Lee family, you have accepted me as family from the very beginning. I'm grateful for your kindness towards me, and hope that we will continue in love. Terry, we did good. Our son represented the best of us. Never forget.

Finally to Cameron Dior Hall in his absence: He will always be my firstborn and muse. Without him, I would not have known motherhood. He is the impetus of this book which has been painful and therapeutic. Had I known then where this life would have brought us, I would have said and done more to show that I love him. "Ms. Lady" has grown a little and I'm okay because the past cannot be undone, yet he will always be my heart.

Peace is a journey of a thousand miles, and it must be taken one step at a time.

Lyndon B. Johnson

Table of Contents

Foreword 1
Chapter 1 – HBCU Glory Days 3
Chapter 2 – Degree Chasing Mother-to-be 15
Chapter 3 – We are the Halls 27
Chapter 4 – Who Holds our Future? 37
Chapter 5 – The Call 39
Chapter 6 – Love Lifted Me 49
Chapter 7 – Who Am I? 57
Chapter 8 – Decisions 61
Chapter 9 – A Stranger Within 67
Chapter 10 – I Am Not the Same 73
Chapter 11 – A Walk in the Dark 77
Chapter 12 – Priorities Matter 91
Chapter 13 – I Don't Want to be in This Club 97
Chapter 14 – The Real Meaning of Life 103
Chapter 15 – The Breaking 113
Chapter 16 – Ugly Firsts 127
Chapter 17 – It's Anger and It's Okay 133
Chapter 18 – Pivotal Change 139
Chapter 19 – Finding A New Normal 145
Chapter 20 – Breathing Again 157
Chapter 21 – Lesson 163
Chapter 22 – The Children 167
Chapter 23 – Forgiveness 173
Chapter 24 – I Am a Witness 179

Foreword

Good ole songs of the sanctified church uplift us. We sing, lift our hands, pat our feet to rhythmic units, and may even shed some tears. These songs speak to us when we cannot utter a word. Lyrics, line after line, prepare us for the days in life when we have to hold on, and do not let go.

> *There's a storm out*
> *On the ocean*
> *And it's moving*
> *This old way*
> *If your soul's not*
> *Anchored in Jesus*
> *You will surely*
> *Drift away…*

Pathway to Peace offers a glimpse into the tapestry of our lives while we share in the perfect imperfection of Jocelyn Hall's memoir. Hope, expectation, disappointment and undeniable suffering leap off the pages to lead others to peace. For "Joyce," the loss of her firstborn son, Cameron, put her on a pathway she never envisioned for herself. In pursuit of peace, she gifts us by baring all to help others navigate through days where nothing makes sense, the fire is too hot, and peace is seemingly unattainable.

This is a guidebook to peace, a roadmap born from Jocelyn's struggles and triumph. While flipping through the pages of her life, we discover the raw, unfiltered truth that resonates with those who wake up into a life they never wanted. Ms. Hall is a master weaver, crafting an inspirational narrative to thrive in the midst of adversity.

Smile. There is a Pathway to Peace.

Kimberly Smith, CEO & Founder
Rivers of Living Water International Ministries
North Carolina, U.S.A.

CHAPTER 1

HBCU Glory Days

"Booyah!" HBCU, here I come!

This was the order of the day as an older teenager about to enter my budding twenties. Truly, the days I would spend at Knoxville College, a Presbyterian school, were the best days of my life. I do not know if it was just the right time, the right place or the right people. Whatever made it work, attending college by stepping into the tradition of a full-on HBCU was more than I ever expected. The experience of an eye-opening education in the company of other students who are valued and protected in the higher education setting was everything HBCUs are made out to be. Entering adulthood as a New Jersey girl temporarily transplanted in Knoxville, Tennessee was my path, and it was a great one.

For every moment of my HBCU college days, I stood among the legacy of graduates who attest to the life-changing experience of going away to college where Black people of the diaspora are the majority of enrolled students. Academic excellence at HBCUs is not exclusionary according to today's rewriting of history. HBCUs are necessary and were founded to curate a higher educational system to answer the race problem in the United States of America. When "negroes" or "coloreds" could not sit side by side at historically white institutions, and were effectively deprived of a college education, our beautiful, brilliant, trailblazing, courageous ancestors were educated at institutions for us and largely, by us.

Historically Black Colleges and Universities were founded to meet a need birthed from white supremacy's hand of exclusion towards the enslaved, and their descendants. Throughout history, HBCUs have been the epicenter of life for Black people to become leaders around the world. Everything about this part of United States history flows like blood through my veins when I reflect upon my days at Knoxville College.

By the early 1980s, during a time that may seem like lifetimes from when HBCUs were founded, my size 9 feet stepped onto campus ready to enter the next phase of life. Technically, my classmates and I were only 6 generations away from slavery and Jim Crow. We were hot off the end of the 60s era. We were bonafide 70s and 80s young adults about to make our impact in the world. Even if we were not one hundred percent sure of how, we were about to do something with our lives and college was the gateway.

Although I came with a "booyah!" in my whole soul, my spirit knew the Lord. I was a church girl who grew up in the sanctified church. Sundays were for church and every day in between belonged to God. Hallelujah to the name of Jesus! I came from the church fellowship days when the chartered buses arrived, and the saints piled our loaded suitcases into the luggage compartment underneath, or the boot. We ought not leave anything we needed between stops in the big suitcases, or we would have to wait until the bus driver pulled up to a rest stop to refuel, or to rest before we could get something we needed. Good packing for the road meant thermoses to keep our drinks hot and coolers to keep our drinks cold. Fried chicken, ham sandwiches, and snacks kept us between rest stops and restaurant breaks until we reached our destinations and returned home. When the saints were not hangry, as in angry because we were hungry, we were less likely to cut up and more likely to sing, play games, prank each other, talk, listen to music, talk the bus driver to death or go to sleep.

Those days seem like yesterday. Ladies had full-fledged holiness gear. Our righteous armor included pantyhose—even if it was hot outside—a slip, and best believe somebody had some safety pins. When we showed up, we were not there to play. Nothing hanging, nothing wiggling all over the place because most of us had a "good" girdle or two to keep our flesh under subjection, literally. Hair rollers, bobby pins, and some thick hair grease were essentials. Road trips, prayer and fasting, choir rehearsal, church anniversaries and conventions meant the church spent a lot of time together. The saints were an extended family with the same spiritual DNA from our Father because we are blood washed through Jesus' sacrificial blood. We spent so much time together, we had to be family.

My strong upbringing by my military father, Joseph Sr, and hard-working mother, Dorothy, was front and center in my constitution. Yet, like many children who go away to college, I was ready to leave my father, mother and only sibling, my younger brother, Joseph Jr. If I were Frick, then Joey had to be Frack. Joey was the Yang to my Ying. We, Frick Frack and Ying Yang, were as close as two siblings could be. Although it was just the two of us, college was calling my name. It was a high time to go to school, and I was blessed to be the first in my immediate family to go away to college.

Knoxville is a small college which was a 12-hour drive from home. The ride from Fort Dix, New Jersey was ample time for my father and mother to drill me as if they had not already prepared me every day of my life for leaving home. All of the years they gave me and Joey a good home were dress rehearsals for the real thing. This time, they had to trust they did a good enough job to drop their daughter off in the Deep South. Once we arrived in the city of Knoxville, Tennessee, my father asked a group of White people how to get to Knoxville College. Those were pull out the Rand McNally map, pre-GPS travel practices. If you did not know how to get from Point A to Point B, you had better stop and ask somebody or drive around in circles for hours. Of course, my parents had no idea how to get to Knoxville College. My mother asked me if I was sure we were in the right place, and my dad assured her we were headed in the right direction. My Dad decided to get a reinforcement opinion, so he pulled up to someone else and asked an African American guy for directions. After following the precise advice full of turns to get to a hill, we arrived at Knoxville College. My journey atop that hill was just beginning.

Once we arrived, I cried and blurted out to my parents, "I don't like it here! I'm gonna die because we're in the projects!" The college looked like it was in the middle of the hood although it was nestled in a housing development. Needless to say, I moved into one of the halls—Brandon Hall—and the first two people I met would be especially important people in my life. They were both sitting in the office of the resident aid. Kecia Jordan asked me if I wanted to be her roommate. Since we were the only two women there, I agreed. Terry Lee was the good Samaritan who volunteered to help my dad unload and put my belongings into my room. That's how my lifelong relationships began with Kecia, my dear friend and forever roommate, and Terry, the young man who would become the father of our son, Cameron.

Once I settled down, the fresh air on the college hill seeped in and I began to breathe a bit easier. After all, being in the South was a complete culture shock for me, an army brat who grew up on Fort Dix, a well-protected and diversely populated army base. Growing up on the base, our family had access to everything. We rarely left the base other than to go to church or to travel on a special trip to see family. Our world was insular, not by choice, but by experience.

The enriching diversity found among Black people from different parts of the country—from around the world—was something new to me and I am better because of it. Being an HBCU student was an eye-opening exposure to Black culture and the diaspora. This was my first encounter with being around mostly Black people. Beforehand, my view was that of base life: full of racial and ethnic diversity in the neighborhood and at school.

My learning curve at Knoxville College was beyond academics. My taste in music went across the board. Salsa, R & B, gospel, mainstream POP, or you name it is what I listened to on the radio, or played on cassettes. As a singer who can more than hum a note, I enjoyed the Police and Patti, Van Halen and Luther, and both Michael's—that is THE Michael Jackson and Michael McDonald. Sade or Chaka, no one could stop the love I had for the world's greatest musical talent. Hall and Oates, Simply Red, Chicago and Foreigner were among my favorites. But at the center of it all were my all-time gospel music favorites like Milton Brunson and the Thompson Community Singers, Chicago Mass Choir, Thomas Whitfield, Keith Pringle, Witness, Commissioned, and the Clark Sisters. Although we still had albums, most of us listened to the radio or had cassettes. We turned up them boom boxes to blast music and sing like we were paid to do it. It wasn't until I got to an HBCU that I began to see the African American experience is more vast that what I had ever seen.

Back in 1983, the college recruited students from heavily Black populated cities like Detroit, Michigan, Cincinnati, Ohio, and of course, Atlanta, Georgia. Our intra-diversity is what made us bond together. Discussions of music, clothing, food, east side, west side, sports loyalties, politics and all sorts of topics made us hold down our own bragging rights. The robust conversations also made us playfully "diss" each other and gravitate towards each other. If you asked me, no one can outdress people from the Northeast. New York, New Jersey, and Philly's (Philadelphia) culture still produces the best fashion trends and styles. Despite these tribal wars, how we truly felt about some of our classmates was much deeper. The few years we were together were the foundation of genuine friendships and relationships which for many of us, would last a lifetime. We ended up like a tight-knit family away from home and often spent breaks and holidays with one another.

Thanksgiving freshman year, I stayed in Knoxville because my parents could not afford the $99 round trip flight. One hundred dollars was pretty expensive for a family on a tight budget. USAir, which later became US Airways, was the main airline that flew into Knoxville, so their flights were the basic options for long distance travel. A school security guard kindly offered Kecia and me Thanksgiving dinner with her family since we were stuck in Knoxville. The gesture was so considerate. But, it was still my first Thanksgiving away from home, and even though there were a lot of friendly faces, I was very lonely with a longing for home. My family celebrated the holidays, and I had a bad case of FOMO aka the fear of missing out while sitting in a stranger's home. I do not remember the officer's name, but she looked out for us like most of the staff at such a small, intimate college. Those of us left behind on an empty campus during the holidays still had somewhere to go because of staff generosity. Being away from my loved ones was part of the aches and pains of growing up.

For the most part, life on campus was exciting. The men became my brothers, and the women became my sisters. In my wildest imaginations, I did not intend to begin my family on campus, but it happened. Terry Lee and I dated during our freshman year. He was a couple of years older than me, and he had an apartment off-campus. By the end of my sophomore year going into my junior year, Terry Lee and I really were not getting along. We decided it was best for us to part ways. But sophomore year, I pledged and became a sorority sister of the Delta Sigma Theta, a member of the Divine 9. Walking the line was involved in the pledging process to earn a rite of passage, so the sorority took up quite a bit of time. Being part of the sorority strengthened my sense of belonging and sisterhood. Yet, it was time to start thinking about junior year and preparing for a career. The emphasis on academic excellence grew stronger. Besides attending classes and student activities, I also traveled with the Knoxville College Concert Choir.

By the time I returned junior year, Terry and I had drifted apart. He was doing his thing, and at that point, I really did not care. But, we had not fully party ways in ways we should have. We were young, and the last thing to go was meeting up with each other.

By today's terms, Terry was far from a sneaky link because we had a history and did care deeply for each other. But, we probably moved into the friends with benefits stage because we were no longer in a committed dating relationship.

In October of 1985, I had a lot of allergies and sinus infections because the leaves, trees and flowers used to do me in every year. I was on birth control pills, but took antibiotics for the sinus infection. The type of antibiotics I was on contradicted the effectiveness of the birth control, so I got pregnant. At the time, I did not even think about whether the medication would make pregnancy a risk. However, I suspected I might be in trouble when my menstrual cycle did not show up. One of my close friends, Angie Walker, and I talked about it, and we decided we should go to the clinic which was towards the back of the campus. Angie had a car, so she drove us to the clinic although it was within walking distance. I asked the nurse for some more birth control pills, but the nurse insisted I take a pregnancy test and it came back positive. I walked outside to Angie's car, and she was sitting there matter-of-factly, awaiting the results. I got in the car, slammed the door and stared with a blank look and cried like a baby. Angie asked, "What is it?"

Sobbing, I said, "I'm pregnant."

As if she needed to hear it again, Angie repeated what I said when she asked, "You're pregnant?"

And I repeated myself and told her again, "I'm pregnant." Through random thoughts rushing through my mind two-steps away from panicking, I told Angie, "I don't know what to do."

Sometimes all you need is one person who believes in you, and will be in your corner. Angie was that person. She said, "Girl, you are gonna have this baby. We are going to be your baby's daddy, don't even worry about it." That assurance came because she knew good and well Terry and I had broken up and we were not together anymore.

A day or two later I braced myself for the conversation with Terry. He needed to know what was going on. The conversation did not go over well. He was not happy that I was pregnant. As a matter of fact, he thought I was lying, and trying to trick him into marriage. I took it a step further and let him know I was not even interested in marrying him and since he did not want to accept the child, there was no pressure. He knew he was my first and only boyfriend and sexual partner. I came to college as a sanctified, holiness church girl and Terry was my first love. His rejection and denial of our son was hurtful, but did not deserve any energy. I was going to be a new mom and had to focus on becoming a mother. So I promised Terry he did not have to worry about me. I would raise the child on my own, but needed to let him know even if he did not believe me. Terry's reaction was just the first in the onset of real pressure. Being pregnant at a Presbyterian college posed other concerns, so Terry Lee was not going to be one of them.

Since I was pregnant, I needed prenatal care. Angie had a car and she gladly took me to every doctor's appointment. Sorors, friends and strangers made sure I was okay. At all times, someone knew exactly where I was, where I was supposed to be, and that I was taken care of. My friends made sure I kept my head lifted high and was never alone. I was in shock but that made me pull myself together to make sure I continued to get excellent grades. The fear of getting kicked out of school and leaving college for good was real. My body was changing, my hormones were changing, and there was pressure all around me. What would my church family think? How was I going to take care of a baby and finish school? Would my mother and father be terribly disappointed in me? Was this baby really going to be fatherless? My parents sent me away to college and my nights were filled with trying to figure out how everything would work out.

CHAPTER 2

Degree Chasing Mother-to-be

It took a while to get adjusted to being pregnant for the first time in my life on campus. Other students may have gotten pregnant, but they did not stay enrolled and attend classes. Most of them packed their bags and left while a handful terminated. I was the only pregnant student on campus and was grateful the president, a dean, and not one school official asked me to leave.

The thing about being pregnant is this: Growing means showing. It's a matter of clockwork and only a matter of time before pregnancy makes a woman's belly bulge. My firstborn was developing when I went home that Christmas. Fool who? Not Dye Hall. My mother's discernment kicked in. She noticed I was eating up a storm and did what mothers do. She gave me a side eye knowing what was going on, but she did not say a word. I just did not have the heart to validate my mom and tell her what was happening. Even though I had exceptional grades and was able to maintain them, the thought of getting kicked out once I began to show or the shame an out-of-wedlock pregnancy brought to my church-going family was overwhelming. That entire Christmas break, I warred within about disappointing my parents. Out-of-wedlock pregnancy was like a slap in their faces after all the years of planning and sacrifice for me to go to college. Then after over-thinking, I wondered how I was going to finish classes and graduate on time. After the holidays, I returned to Tennessee with a baby bump and began "to show."

Well, the school administration and professors may have gotten wind of my situation through the grapevine, but they did not interfere with my educational pursuits. At the time, Dr. Clinton Marsh was President of Knoxville College. The college administrators, staff and faculty did not mention a thing to me. In fact, the college overlooked their liability in allowing me to stay in-residence at a dorm. I should have been kicked off campus, but they were all extremely helpful in making sure I was good. The only setback was a sit-down. The school choir master relayed I could not travel with the choir anymore. My pregnancy was not a good look for the traveling choir. The President of Knoxville College—a Christian institution—leveraged the choir for campaign fundraising efforts. We sang at several White Presbyterian churches across the country, and they used to send us back to Knoxville College with considerable benefactor funding. Although I sang with the choir for a few years, the illustrious director, Miss Ruth B. Stokes, told me I could not sing anymore. To put it bluntly, she told me I was a liability. I understood and although it was a downer, there was no pushback. Some things we may not like and would even do differently if the shoes were on our feet. My heart hurt, because singing was something I enjoyed. But, being pregnant was not something that fit with the image the school choir portrayed. The dismissal was about interests bigger than me, so I took the loss. My concern was to get my college degree with my newfound brothers and sisters. I could not dodge the pregnancy anymore. There had to be a way to break the news to my parents.

It is hard to imagine anyone chipper and so overjoyed telling her parents she is pregnant when her parents sent her away to go to college. At least in my world, the news was not something I wanted to break to my parents. It may have been easier if the phone call was going to be, "Mom, guess what? I know you did not plan for me to become a mother this way, but I am pregnant. Terry and I are very happy about it, and we are going to do our best to take care of our child." Or, even if the presentation was Terry and I were still a couple and had a hiccup in getting pregnant before marriage. In my head and heart, that may have come across better. Despite all the pros and cons, what ifs and what not's, I was out there all by myself and there was no turning back. Somewhere around February or March of my junior year, I had to make a telephone call to tell my parents the "good" news. Back in those days, the saints wanted some sort of public performance for sin atonement. Having a baby outside of marriage was nothing to brag about.

I got on the payphone and dialed home, collect. For all the post payphone born people, this means when I went to a public pay phone and picked up the telephone, I did not put in any coins to pay for and make the call. An intermediary person or automated system took a recording of my name, and called my parents' home phone line. She picked up, and heard an automated message with my name "Joyce" inserted in it, and accepted the collect phone charges which would appear on the monthly phone bill. My mom answered the phone, approved the collect call charges, and I announced, "You know. I got something to tell you."

My mom asked what it was, and I told her I was having a baby. She already had a hunch I was pregnant, so she was ready. She said, "Well, whatever you do, don't get rid of the baby. We are gonna make it work. We are gonna raise this child, and we're gonna make it work."

Whew. It is possible to feel two things at the same time. On the one hand, I felt relieved! My mom knew, it was finally over! Without knowing what she thought would be best, the logistics did not even matter. My mother was accepting and assured me she was right by my side; my baby would be fine. Also, I was disappointed in myself. My mom was my biggest cheerleader if "Joyce, go to college and get a good education" was a team. My mom was proud of me for doing what she could not do.

Dorothy Hall was a huge proponent of me pursuing higher education because when she was growing up, my maternal grandfather did not want to send her off to college, even though she had a full ride. My mom had an athletic scholarship yet my grandfather, who successfully farmed land, told my mom she could not go. He needed her to work on the farm and stay in the fields. The same young woman who had to forego a college education wanted me to have the opportunity she did not. My full ride to Knoxville College meant so much to my mom and I always understood how blessed I was to have access to higher education. Ms. Dye was ready to put in the work to help me finish. If my parents ever withstood any sort of backlash for stepping up to help me with the pregnancy, they have never mentioned it. As far as I knew, all I had to do was get my college degree. Jocelyn Hall, Joseph and Dorothy's daughter, had to cross the finish line and complete what she began.

Because I was so far away from home, I went through all the stereotypical changes that come along with pregnancy without my mom. The number one craving I had was for potatoes and sour cream. My roommate and I had a refrigerator, hot plate and a hot pot in the dorm room. Kecia and I would boil potatoes and when they were done, we'd put some butter and sour cream on them. For the most part, we managed all of the cravings right in the dorm room. Getting around on campus required more energy because I gained quite a bit of weight and walked to and from class on the hill. I did as much as I could and so many students made me feel seen and safe.

The Omega Psi Phi fraternity had their lamps, also known as their line pledgees. One day, I was in the library, and a pledgee came over and told me he was instructed to rub my ankles. He politely leaned down and took my legs and massaged my ankles and feet. That brother did not understand what he did for me that day. A few other lamps found me from time-to-time and massaged my legs. The lamps also escorted me to and from class, because by the end of the pregnancy, I was wobbling around with swollen ankles.

Although I was not singing with the choir anymore, the college allowed me to travel with them to Washington, D.C. for a performance. My parents drove to meet us. This was the first time my parents had seen me since I had called them on the phone and told them. I was about six months pregnant when I saw my parents and I could not hold back the tears. My mother comforted me and said, "It is going to be alright." My father did not talk too much. His presence said what it needed to say to me. When it came to raising my brother and me, my father was never too vocal about things. My mother was more interactive. Once again, she let me know everything was still okay. By the end of my junior year when my parents came to pick me up, I was eight months pregnant and a few weeks away from the delivery date.

By the summer of '86, I was back at home and ready to deliver. Heat and pregnancy do not mix. It was a hot summer and seemed hotter than most because being too hot when pregnant was extremely uncomfortable. It was not long before my son was ready to make his entrance into the world. On July 31, 1986, at 1:13

AM after 13 hours of labor with the God-sent help of an epidural, I gave birth to Cameron Dior Hall. My mom and one of my aunts, affectionately known as Aunt Jack, were in the delivery room with me and they saw everything. My aunt made some remarks about Cameron's big head and what it did to my privates, but there was nothing I could say. After being in labor for that long, I could not care any less how big his head was, just as long as he was out and it was over! Cameron finally arrived and everything changed.

It was a joy and an honor to be a mother and I took that position in life seriously. My baby boy was named "Cameron Dior Hall." His name was a combination of Chancen Dior, a newborn from a local Knoxville couple that I knew through Kecia. The name Chancen had such a beautiful regal tone. Although I did not take the exact name outright, I played around with the first name and came up with "Cameron." Christian Dior was one of the luxury designer brands to flex during those times, so I adopted the same middle name, "Dior." Cameron Dior is a strong name, one that I knew no one would ever forget. I was a junior in college when he was born, and I was determined that we would make this journey of life full of love and great memories. He was perfect in my eyes. My eyes gazed at him, knowing that the two of us would make it as a family. Thankfully, I have a small family and everyone was all in to make sure Cameron would have a rich life.

The last year of college was on the horizon. The last thing I wanted to do was to extend my graduation date. So I took some classes to stay on track. My mother had a plan and about one month after

Cameron was born, she sat me down for a long conversation. At the turning point of the information age, Email communication, the digital age, or the world wide web, the path of life for success was transitioning. My family was still of the belief that in order to be successful, to get ahead in life, or to be able to make it, after high school, you better find yourself in somebody's college or university, trade school or apprenticeship program, or the military. When I went to college, I was the hope of my family. But I had a little too much fun coming of age and then came home without the reliable support of his father. I expressed my concern about graduating. Ms. Dye said, "Oh no! We are going to get you graduated. Whatever happens, you will be graduating on time!"

My mother's take was whatever viewpoints others espoused did not write the script. Together, we would craft our own destiny with God's help. Between my mom and my goals, Cameron was going to be well cared for, and intentionally loved. My entrance to motherhood included my mother's support to make sure I would be able to give Cameron a good life. The plane had already taken off, the ship was already mid-sea and had not arrived at its destination. My mother decided that until I finished school and began working, she would step up to nurture Cameron. I was relieved, nervous and excited at the same time. At least I got to go back to school, but that meant I had to leave Cameron. As a new mom, it was scary to think my newborn would not see my face or know my touch. My mother took the responsibility of caring for him while I went back to school to get my college degree. If anyone had to care for Cameron, she was the one to do it. The same woman who raised me was more than capable of giving Cameron a great start in life. We agreed that in the upcoming January, I would head back to Knoxville.

Meanwhile, for the first five months of Cameron's life, my mom and I cared for Cameron. Since we agreed it would be best to finish school, I called an advisor at Knoxville College to see what I could do to stay on track for graduation. All I needed was a statistics class, so I took a stats and a business law class at the College of New Jersey, formerly Trenton State College, to lighten the load when I went back down South. I used welfare payments for those night courses so I would not fall behind. Twice a week, I traveled to Trenton and hung out with my cousin Gloria during the day until it was time for class. My mother was a working woman in the paid labor force, so taking care of her grandson was surely a labor of love.

In January of 1987, it was time to go back to Knoxville. I stood in the Philadelphia International Airport and wept like a baby because after all the preparation, I was still not ready to leave Cameron. He would be in the most perfect hands with my parents, but I still was not ready. It was time to go back to campus which was not the same because motherhood makes everything different. Although I had a relatively easy pregnancy medically speaking, it was difficult because of the trauma of being on a college campus where everyone knows your most obvious business. Most people knew I was "caught out there," knowing who the father was, and that he had nothing to do with me since he found out I was pregnant. Terry Lee did come to see Cameron when he was born, and once he laid eyes upon him, there was no doubt he was the father. He did not need a Jerry Springer DNA test, no one did. It was as if God said let's make Cameron look just like Terry Lee so all doubt will be removed. And it was. My hope was that Terry Lee and I would be able to move on from the awkwardness and become good at coparenting.

The reality of having a child, another human with my DNA who relied upon me to be his mom was setting in. Cameron was a few weeks shy of 6 months old, and the next 6 months seemed like an eternity. My mom did her best to make sure he could hear my voice when we spoke over the telephone, but my heart ached to hurry up and graduate. Every day, my motivation was my son. And, I wanted to be able to take care of him so my mom could get back to her life. Terry Lee and I—after pulling some of his teeth— had to give my mother temporary custody of Cameron so she could participate in programs like WIC and Medicaid to get baby formula and to cover doctor visits. At first, Terry Lee did not understand why we had to grant my mom temporary custody. He thought we were trying to trick him to take Cameron away from him. He called my mother and after speaking with her, he reluctantly agreed. My mother did the heavy lifting for us and there was no way she deserved aggravation when all she wanted to do was do her best to take care of Cameron on a tight budget.

Those six months were exhausting and rough knowing that my son was elsewhere. Yes, my child was also his grandparents' joy. Cameron was with my parents and my brother, but I was missing in his day-to-day life. The focus was to be strong and do what needed to be done so we could still have a great future. We had a lifetime ahead of us. My family sacrificed to make sure we had a good head start. As much as I missed Cameron, the longing helped me to tighten up so I could have a fresh start once I graduated and moved back home for good.

By June of 1987, it was time to graduate! I did it, right? Not entirely. Although I was the student enrolled in classes and obtained the degree, every step I took towards graduation were on the heels of my ancestors who paved the way for a young Black woman to get an education, and especially my mother's. Quitting was not an option. Dorothy Hall made sure her daughter did not have to quit. My mother, father and brother loved their grandson and nephew and took care of him so that I could walk across the stage and get my diploma signifying a bachelor's degree in accounting, and flip my tassel. I made it. We made it!

My family traveled to Tennessee for the commencement exercises and all I remember is being excited to see Cameron again. My heart nearly dropped out of my chest when I reached for him and he did not know who I was; He cried when I tried to hold him and reached for my parents. I was terrified and wondered if I made a mistake by going back to Knoxville instead of staying at home with him in New Jersey. My mother, in the meantime, told me to calm down and relax. It was perfectly natural for Cameron to be more attached to them, but he was my child. He belonged solely to me. The separation was over, and Cameron would gravitate to me, his mother.

For the couple of days Cameron was on campus, my friends and others noticed and adored him. All we heard were statements like, "Oh my God, he looks just like Terry Lee," or "Look at Terry Lee!" The situation was terribly awkward. I would reach out to Cameron and he would not find comfort in me. He looked at me like, *who are you?* He crawled all over my mom, father, and Joey, but he would not come anywhere near me. I started to have a panic attack. As usual, my mother gave me wisdom. She said he will come around sooner than we think. After all, the baby I left was growing. He was 11 months old and walking. He was fat, pudgy and perfectly cute nestled in the comfort of those who cared for him, his family, my family. He was growing and no longer the newborn who was born with extra pinky fingers. They had no feeling in them—while I swore that had to have been his daddy's genes—yet the doctors told us to tie them, they would fall off and they did. Nonetheless, Cameron woke up to consistent faces and he was way too young to process my feelings. Truth be told, so was I. It never dawned on me that my baby would not know me when I had been away at school for more than half of his developmental life at 11-months-old. It took a few weeks, but after being around consistently, Cameron knew his mama. I could breathe again.

CHAPTER 3

WE ARE THE HALLS

We plan, God laughs. Our plans do not work, God listens. We seek God first, He is pleased.

This is what I learned about God from an incredibly young spiritual age. Lord knows, God listened and heard my cries when I brought home a young baby as part of my college experience. When I settled back in New Jersey, everyone accepted Cameron with open arms. If there was gossip or resistance, I was not aware of it. Of course, there was some buzzing going around, like buzzards ready to feed off a dead carcass. But I was alive. All was well, and since no one verbalized anything to me personally, I minded my business. And Cameron was my business.

My parents, Joe and Dye, are the core of my existence. They gave my brother, Joe Jr. aka Joey, and I a meaningful childhood growing up in the 1960s, 70s, and 80s. They supported me through many activities–from ballet, softball, and basketball to all around scholastics. A major motivation in life has been to make them happy because of all their love for me and my brother. To be quite frank, it was not until I went away to college and left the military installation that I realized how much of a Leave-It-to-Beaver-like family we have. My parents were not perfect people or perfect parents. But they sure did give us a home that I took for granted. I had no idea that everyone did not have two parents, may have never known a parent, or were brought up in abusive situations. When I left the nest, self-awareness woke me up to how sheltered I was. Once I became a young mom while still enrolled in college, my parents became grandparents. That is when I saw the depth of their love for me. I thought I knew it before. But having a child while I was unmarried and away at school in Tennessee made me witness my parents stepping up to parent me and my firstborn while I became a young mom. They made sure I did not fail.

Like most single mothers, I worked and took care of Cameron. The family enjoyed him as he grew up and we began—as the old folks say—to see his personality come in. We attended church and I kept in touch with Kecia, Angie and my sorors, who were like sisters. It is true. Some college relationships last a lifetime. My college buddies and I went to different geographic locations and kept in touch as we started our careers. After years of solidarity with my college friends, life looked a little different than it was before I left home to go to college. Adulting meant we had to figure out how to be long distance friends as all of us moved on with our lives. The process was especially challenging since my buddies, my friends, had been my immediate support system for years.

Romance and the "love life" was a dud. Partly, because I had to focus on settling down and standing on my own two feet with a child. More so, it was because I turned down a marriage proposal from Terry Lee. He did propose at graduation. Although I did care for him deeply, I could not see us in a successful marriage after his reaction to my pregnancy with Cameron. Terry had settled down in Knoxville, Tennessee and we lived in different states. However, we were forging a better understanding of one another as parents to our blessing. Terry was welcome to see his son whenever he desired, my home was open to him. Just because we were no longer a couple did not mean Terry and Cameron's relationship should be affected.

Once I had my second son, DeMaris, the three of us were one tight family. Life was not a fairytale, yet life was good. Life was basic, sort of like complete without the frills. My boys, Cameron and DeMaris, and I had an amazingly simple life. Our days were full of ups and downs, but the days were surely ours. If a heartbeat sounds like "whishh, shhhhhh," Cameron was my whishh and Demaris was my shhhhh. My boys were not equally loved; They have been wholly loved in their own right. There's nothing equal about this kind of love. My heart and the love it gives has never been divided regarding them. When God gave us to each other, they were etched into a mother's love all their own. My sons Cameron Dior and Demaris Stephen are the epitome of my love.

My approach to giving my two sons a good life was not about the Benjamins or the Johnsons. It was about the Halls, doing the best we could with what we had. And my boys made that part of being a mother easy. My goals were to keep them in church to learn about God, earn enough money to afford a home, provide insurance, put healthy meals on the table, make sure they had a good education and leave them an inheritance when I pass on. Most of all, if I did well with them, they would be kind, thoughtful human beings who love life, and know how to cherish it. The list seems out of pocket for a single mom, but I have always believed it is attainable. My mom and dad gave their parents homage by going further than they did, and I was positioned to do the same with an accounting degree. My father gave me gold mine advice which made me chase stability, consistency, and reliable growth career-wise. When I was out of college and my father strongly recommended that I work for the government. He said, "You'll always have a job with the government. They'll never go broke or lay you off." Now even though the government can go broke and has hiring freezes and layoffs, my father's advice stuck with me. For the most part, a strong long career in the federal sector is reliable and that is what I needed to take care of my boys. It is one thing to have to take care of myself. I could have easily roughed it and figured things out with a knapsack on my back, two changes of clothes, and some willing friends to bounce between for a while if things got tough. But once I became a mother, two children looked to me with every confidence they would be secure. My determination was to make sure consistent money was coming in and my life choices have been centered around what is best for them. With God's help, my boys, through a path all their own, were going to go farther than me. At least that was the plan.

Quite a few people thought it would be good to venture out of my comfort zone and move someplace else. New Jersey is the nucleus of my immediate family, so it made sense to stay around. I didn't want to relocate or change jobs because my children needed stability. Their uncle, Joey, was right there and he has always acted as if he is their authority figure, to my irritation and their aggravation. Nonetheless, he has been the ace uncle who would do anything for his nephews as if they were his own. Also, with the benefits of earning personal time, weekends and holidays off, it seemed right to stay put and raise my children. I had a good job without any concern that it would be a workable fit since I did have children. Dad's advice has proven to be true. I'm thirty years plus in as a manager with the department of the Navy. Most of all, my parents have always loved my children as if they were theirs. Although my boys and I were a family, we have always had an extended family where they have had the love, care and the influence of their grandparents. As an intergenerational unit, we were incredibly basic.

My parents helped when I needed a sitter so I could work to take care of my children. There is no way I could have handled the demands if my parents were not all in. When I had out of town business meetings or needed financial support to make ends meet, my parents made sure I did not fall short. My brother helped out when he could and my sons treated him more like an older brother than an uncle. Through the highs and lows of parenting, we made it.

There were weekends when I had to go to work. As a working mom, it would have been nice to have weekends off. But when we had to go in to work, my boys got up and went right along with me. My co-workers embraced my little fellas as their own and the boys knew each of my co-workers by name. My boys were so much a part of the work family one of my colleagues adopted them as her grandsons. Every Christmas and birthday, she made sure our boys had gift certificates to McDonald's. Back in the day, McDonald's was a treat, especially if the kiddie meal had a popular toy out. Those gift certificates were a treat.

As a family, we maximized our weekends. When Cameron and Demaris were younger, Saturdays and Sundays were filled with good food and football. Now, it could be said that I am into football because of my kids, but that would be far from the whole truth. My kids were born to a sports mom, so they got their zeal for sports honestly. Yes, I was that mom. I made sure that my boys were sports enthusiasts. Our sports-loving family enhanced my experience as a mother. Even though my kids loved sports for themselves, it was definitely something we had in common. Watching the games was our dedicated time together. No one could tell us a thing when it came to our fandom! Cameron and I were diehard Philadelphia Eagles fans, especially when it came to football. Demaris decided to be an Atlanta Falcons fan. I have no idea to this day where I went wrong with that, but he is his own man and has his own loyalties. The Falcons? In any case, you could hear us in the streets screaming at every touchdown made, fumble recovery, and bad referee call. We were that crew–ten toes down ready to defend our teams! There were many times where our living room was just as fan crazy as the stands in a stadium. We were on time, lit and got to the point where we came to the television with our sports memorabilia. If social media had been a thing back then, we probably would have gone viral.

My boys and I knew how to roll with it and nobody knew that we were struggling as much as we did from time to time. Growing up, my little fellas wore tees, jeans, and sneakers. They were very content and didn't complain when what I could afford was not a top brand. They had enough swag to make Walmart look like Macy's. Hamburger Helper was the meal when the money was tight and a trip to Red Lobster's was our treat when times were good.

There were some sketchy moments when I fell behind and had to rob Peter to pay John. They happened more than I had hoped, but it was hard to catch up sometimes. We were locked out of our apartment a few times and had to go to court. It was embarrassing and hard to digest when a full-time job still was not enough to get ahead. Yet we did our best to enjoy what we had.

Some of my fondest memories of spending time with my boys were when we traveled along the east coast to visit my parents who had relocated to Virginia or attended our family vacation in Myrtle Beach. We used to road trip down I-95 or Route 13 and blast all sorts of music. The boys and I are from different generations so even though we loved music, we preferred artists from our times. We blasted Criss-Cross, the Isley Brothers, Floetry, Jill Scott and Musiq Soulchild to name a few. Before we knew it, we were almost to our destination. My boys enjoyed road trips, even quick one day trips around the New Jersey, Philadelphia or Delaware tri-state area. They were adventurous and stayed ready to do something new. And they loved the challenge of directing our way back home after paying close attention to the routes we traveled.

On Sundays, Cameron, Demaris and I went to church. Jesus has always been the reason, so despite our busy schedules, we set aside Sundays to make sure we worshipped the Lord with the fellowship of the saints. Jesus is the center of our lives, of it all, so being at a place where we could hear a preached word and worship was essential. Plus, they needed a sense of belonging. Our church family has always been an extended family.

My sons grew up like a lot of Black families with good gospel music playing at home, in the car, or sung in church and just about anywhere. We listened to gospel music artists like Commissioned, Lamar Campbell, Mary Mary, and anything Kirk Franklin to uplift our souls. Those precious times were what made the Hall boys. Weekends were spent driving to no particular destination, just time for us. They were taught about being aware of their surroundings, and learned how to travel to and from. They looked for landmarks or anything that would remind them of which way they came in order to navigate their way back to la casa. Both of my boys had great instinct and could lead us back home the same way they came.

Like a lot of unmarried moms, taking care of my boys was the key focus of my life. There were many things I had to sacrifice as a single mom, and one thing that was intentional was to screen my personal relationships. Although I desired to have a husband, my children had to be part of a new family if I were to ever marry. Otherwise, I made my relationship status work for what was best for the three of us. Things and people can come and go. But my boys would always be there! No way under God's heaven could "uncles" be floating around, in and out of my life, and around my boys for obvious reasons. They already had fathers, a grandfather, and uncles. Too much was at stake to allow them to be emotionally connected to someone who was more temporal than permanent. Making the necessary sacrifices for my children's safety was not a hard thing to do. Keeping them out of harm's way was extremely important. It was not always easy, but putting their needs before mine was non-negotiable.

Parents dream. We dream for our children until they can dream for themselves. And even when they do, some of us want to proofread their dreams until they are old enough to exercise veto power. *Huh? Are you sure about that? I've been down that road, trust me, you do not want to go there! Son, didn't you hear anything I've taught you? Do you think this is God-approved? Maybe you should wait a little while longer. Son, that's a trap! Okay, how can we make this happen? Are you ready? Have you considered the costs and consequences? Is this what you want for yourself? Let's plan wisely.*

With motherhood comes a reckoning that as much as our instincts guide us, there is a time when boys become men. All of our plans, special moments, hopes, and dreams for them—or with them—is not something we control. Their self-determination is not ours to give. Neither is the day when they are called out of this world and we are left blindsided. For parents who have suffered through the loss of a child, our forever babies who the psyche is meant to believe will outlive us, we know when our children leave us, so does a part of our hearts. For me, when Cameron left—when someone murdered him, when someone cut his life short, and when someone almost killed my soul—the peace of God that I had known for every day of my existence seemed to disappear, too. I found myself in a whirlwind and when the damage was done and things began to settle, I was so broken that it was hard to make it through the day. I may have appeared to be the same person, but the brutal murder of my son changed who I am. Everything changed. Every day thereafter, when I opened my eyes there was a pathway before me: a pathway to peace.

CHAPTER 4

Who Holds our Future?

Parents tend to hope for a bright future and everything they expect their children to be. We do not plan to outlive our children or to ever stand before them, mourning their loss of life. For as long as they have been lent to me, because God chose my womb to be their place of Creation and me to be their mother, my boys and I have been three-corded in love.

When Cameron was taken from his loved ones, our family and his dearest friends found ourselves in a place we never conceptualized. Planning for tragedy and dreaming of child loss by murder is something that never even crossed my mind. Sure, there were times when I had concerns about something tragic happening to my sons, after all, they are Black young men in America. Yet, those were fleeting thoughts that did not dictate the life they were going to live. My hopeful heart had the "best of" written all over it for the lives my sons and I would live. Great things were in store for us. What? I was a praying woman. My faith did not lead me to any outcome where death, especially a murder, would stop my boys from seeing their hopes and dreams come to pass, firsthand. My sons were raised in church, just like their uncle, my only sibling, and I were. Despite life's ups and downs, we had every confidence that God would give us a good life, a prosperous life. Even as our souls prospered, we would all live with temptations, trials, and testing. But, death? The finality of death at such a young age was not in the plan.

In all of the things I thought was necessary to teach the boys, there was never a day when I planned for a tragedy that we, with the help of God, could not overcome together. A child of God, one who lives by faith, one who fasted and prayed, was not "supposed" to wake up into a day when my son would be taken from this world. Cameron was still young at 26 years old. He still had the rest of his life ahead of him. Sure, life has its ups and downs. Of course, people are murdered and pass away unexpectedly from many causes. Surely there are evil things that happen in a world that we cannot always control. But my son was covered. He had been surrounded by praying people for every moment of his life. My plans and the great expectation I had for his life were no more. Abruptly, the day came when everything changed. That day disrupted everything about life as I knew it. My son lost his life, and that day, his murder brought me to the crossroads of losing and regaining peace. His death has, to some degree, challenged my family's faith and identity. It has ushered us to the threshing floor, and taken our knees and faces to the ground. As a loving mother, knowing my son's life was brutally taken from him caused pain like no other. My family wrestled with our emotions, reality, and God.

CHAPTER 5

THE CALL

For I reckon that the sufferings of this present time are not worthy to be compared with the glory which shall be revealed in us. - Romans 8:18

This hello is not the hello I want to hear

There are momentous times in life, the events that happen that we will never forget. Birthdays, first loves, first cars, first homes, proposals and engagements, weddings, anniversaries, family reunions, or the announcements of a growing family are the moments we cherish and want to remember. Nowadays, before we move onto baby showers, there may just be a gathering for close friends and loved ones to come and see what gender the new baby is going to be. Gender reveals are popular, but they still don't outshine the days our precious babies are born. For mothers, we usually recall everything that it takes to bring a human life into this world. Parents and loved ones can typically celebrate the little things like when our babies lift their heads on their own, roll over, crawl, take their first few steps, say their first words, and smile with one tooth bursting through their gums. We may recall the first day we have to go back to work and leave them in someone else's care or have to watch them strut their little legs with all the confidence they can muster to walk into a classroom with a new teacher and students. For me, my hope was for Cameron to become a god-fearing man, to know the good news of the gospel of Jesus Christ, and His saving grace. With everything we experience in life, that would be the most momentous moment for my son so that everything else would have a God-given, God-intended purpose in his life. My prayers were for Cameron to answer the call of God.

Seemingly, there was an interruption to my plans, and the plan of God according to my faith. On July 12, 2013, at around 9:30 am, a moment that was never supposed to take place happened. The day began as a regular Friday. As I have always done, I got up and got ready for another workday. It was time to enjoy the weekend. I was looking forward to meeting up with friends in Washington, DC for the upcoming Delta Sigma Theta sorority centennial celebration. I was just waiting to get my day going at work, and hoped it was going to be an easy day. Up until that time, nothing was out of the ordinary, yet I saw a number on my cell that I did not recognize. Normally, I would not have answered the call. But for some reason, this time, I did. On the other end of the phone I heard the words, "Mom, I am so sorry."

Not knowing what there was to be sorry about, I just said, "Sorry about what?" I recognized Candice's voice as one of Cameron's friends who also lived in Stockbridge, Georgia.

I curiously asked, "Did Cam get in trouble?" At first, I thought that Cameron had gotten into some trouble. We had been through this before, so I did not get excited. Not that bad, right?

Since Candice and her brother, Gill, were Cameron's roommates, I did not think anything major when she called. Cameron wanted to relocate to Georgia after finding out he had a daughter. He wanted to be closer to his baby girl so moved in with Candice and Gill since they had all known each other and been friends when they were growing up in New Jersey. Although Candice said she was sorry, all I wanted clarity about what she was sorry about. She repeated, "Mom, I am so sorry."

Now this time, I was more alert because she repeatedly told me the same thing about being sorry. Then Candice gave me the news. "Mom, Cameron is dead."

At that moment, an experience like never before invaded my being. Once those words registered, hearing them was like a vortex sucking the very life out of me. I could not breathe and the only words I could say was, "Oh my God."

Those repeated words became louder and louder and my co-worker asked what was wrong. I could barely whisper and told him my son was dead. Like a flash, I had co-workers rushing into my office as I was trying to catch my breath. My focus, and my thoughts were flooded with grasping the reality of what Candice said. One of the first results of hearing the news was nothing was making sense. I grasped for anything that could help me regain my equilibrium. *How and why could this happen? My firstborn? Why! Oh my God!*

The news left me in shock. It felt as if I were out of my own body looking at television and I was in the middle of the nightmare wondering when all of this would end. *Could this be a cruel joke?* Just shy of passing out, I kept trying to rationalize what I heard. Nothing made sense with questions flooding me faster than I could breathe or think. Yet with little information, I still had to inform my family.

My family, which consisted of my parents, brother, and my only surviving son, DeMaris, were all that I had. How in the world was I going to call them with the terrible news? I called my friend who was a pastor and pleaded with him to call my brother Joe, because at that point, I was seconds from being utterly hysterical. I hung up from him and called my son's father, Terry, who still lived in Tennessee. That was the hardest phone call to place. After all, Cameron and his dad were just building a relationship and Cameron decided to move Down South to connect. This was a prayer I always had for them so I was happy to encourage our son to move to be closer to this dad. I do not know why, but I kept apologizing repeatedly when I broke the news. Some part of me felt like I had let his father down because his opportunity to be closer to Cameron was gone. Terry gasped and I heard the sense of despair from a father who lost his only son. Terry and Cameron had just started to rebuild their relationship and with the news of Cameron's passing, there would not be an opportunity for what they both hoped. Although they were on good terms for a few months when Cameron decided to relocate to Georgia in March of 2012, I was optimistic that Cameron and Terry would be the best of friends. They were going to share ideas, have meaningful conversations, and do what men do. When I had spent years praying for this reunion between my son and his father. *Why now God? When things were getting better for us all, why was death here?*

Part of me also died that day when I answered the phone call. Every dream, smile, and moment with my firstborn and our future died that day. What I had hoped for in my firstborn stopped. From the time Cameron drew his first breath, I was optimistic for him. Without any warning, time to try to figure it out, or time to pray our way out, Cameron and everything attached to his living died. Before I realized I would never hear Cameron's voice again, I rushed home to get to DeMaris, my youngest son. Even though I was devastated and it all felt like a bad dream, my instinct was to hurry up and be there for my baby boy. When I walked into the house, he was sitting on the floor in tears, because he had already been informed before I had a chance to tell him. Just looking at his face tore my heart to pieces. It made me cry harder knowing that this was now our reality. What was happening was unreal. It was not something we had in the possibilities of life manual.

Murder?

Cameron?

My brother, Joe, was also at the house and he had a sheepish look, as if he were lost. With every ounce of courage Joey uttered, "I know, I know." He did know. After all, Cameron was like a son to him. DeMaris lost his big brother, who was also like a father to him. My parents lost a grandson who they regarded as their own son. We all lost Cameron, and began to experience grief about what Cameron lost: his life. He was robbed of his human existence. We all had to endure this pain separately and corporately. I was surrounded by devastation and wondered how we were going to survive this, but had to come to terms with Cameron's untimely passing. Even though it felt as if I died when that call came in, the reality was I was alive. I was still a child of God. When I did not have any sense of what to expect next, and was finding out what real heartbreak is, my inner man took control and declared, "Lord I trust you." That's all I heard come out of my heart to God. After all, I believed God in all things but this was different. The challenge was to hold onto what I know about faith and walking with God. The challenge was to live while believing God in death. Through all of the disappointment and pain, God is still God.

Growing up in church, it is instinctual to know all the right words to say and what to pray. I was a good Christian with the hope of seeing God when that great day would come—for me. I was living to live again! We used to sing Albert E. Brumley's good ole hymn of the church.

I'll Fly Away

Some glad morning when this life is o'er,
I'll fly away;
To a home on God's celestial shore,
I'll fly away (I'll fly away).

Chorus
I'll fly away, Oh Glory
I'll fly away; (in the morning)
When I die, Hallelujah, by and by,
I'll fly away (I'll fly away).

When the shadows of this life have gone,
I'll fly away;
Like a bird from prison bars has flown,
I'll fly away (I'll fly away)

Chorus
Just a few more weary days and then,
I'll fly away;
To a land where joy shall never end,
I'll fly away (I'll fly away)

When I sang this and other songs of the glorious days when the saints will go to our eternal home, nothing in my constitution had the roads we may have to take to see Jesus face to face. For all the years of looking for the blessed hope and glorious reappearing of my Lord and Savior, Jesus Christ, there was only eternal joy in my heart. Whether we pass away in this life, or see the reappearing of our Lord, there was never a sense of crushing or brutal pain to transition into our eternal life. Song after song, eternal hope and promise, and nothing could fix what the family had to face each day.

"Some glad morning, when this life is over, I'll fly away."

The only trouble is Cameron's life was not supposed to be over. Just when he began to stand ten toes down in his manhood, he died and I wanted God to fix it quickly. He had to bring my child back! It was not time for my son to fly away! Cameron was my flesh and blood, the one I gave birth to during my junior year in college. He was my ride or die and with DeMaris, they were the only reasons why I even existed on the earth. I didn't care how much trouble he'd previously experienced; I was his mother–the one who loved him the most for every moment of his life. What child would not think that the love of the mother is the best in the world? Cameron had that parent, so I thought.

I wasn't prepared to experience life without Cameron. Parents rarely imagine a life without their children even when they leave home, get married, have children, and grow old. Most may hope their adult children remember to call, text, and visit often. We always want to be a part of their lives, as they have been a pivotal part of ours. My hope was to see Cameron happy as he made a life for himself, and began his own family. Despite tough times, and all sorts of events we got through, this new revelation—losing Cameron—was our reality. Our firstborn died and it meant a permanent separation in this life, and took all of our breaths away. Each of us died that day. We had to live out this nightmare. Without warning, we had to walk this journey alone. All of us had these painful faraway expressions trying to gather some rationale for what just took place.

At that point of brokenness and fragility, it seemed as if chaos was everywhere. Chaos within ripped through my very being. While having to make arrangements for Cameron's passing, we had to interact with law enforcement and the judicial system. When it seemed as if there was not one more thing I could deal with, I learned a valuable lesson. My tribe was the first in line to hold me up.

CHAPTER 6

LOVE LIFTED ME

The news of Cameron's passing spread quickly. Before I could gather thoughts, or leave work to get home, family, friends, and loved ones flooded my house. My church family were among those who left work, stopped what they were doing and within an hour or two, showed up to my home. There were so many people who loved Cameron and wanted to support our family, that there was not enough room inside. But that did not stop some from staying outdoors. My tribe was right there.

There's a saying that a true friend who loves you in life, will treasure you in death. When I looked around and saw our family friends, some who had to sit on the floor, they were in shock and disbelief. They wept, and some were silent. Most of all, they were present. My tribe gave me strength by the gift of their presence. Within the first couple of hours and the ensuing days is when my tribe showed up strongly. They were my everything. There were moments when I felt like I was going to pass out, but the support kept me grounded.

Terry and his wife, Robin, traveled from Tennessee to New Jersey. By the time they arrived, they were shocked by the number of people who came by to offer condolences, prayer, good wishes, and a listening ear. We had food for weeks. In that moment, a tribe can make or break you. Cameron's friends showed up. And so did Demaris' co-workers and his support system. So many people made sure they were there to catch us so we did not fall.

In the midst of the news, and immediate need to make plans, we all had questions that to this day have not been fully answered.

Why?

What happened?

Who did this?

There was only so much I could do, and I had to make decisions. One decision was to make sure I did not crack, or snap in succumbing to the pressure and pain. Wisdom stepped in and said there are some things I was not ready to handle. So although we did have to cooperate with law enforcement, Terry took the lead.

Based on the police report, Cameron was found in a cul-de-sac in the suburbs of Atlanta stabbed multiple times. Had he been found earlier, he would have lived. A resident in that area found him lying in their front yard on their way to work. It was 4 AM when the police got the call. Another resident said that earlier in the evening, they heard a car beeping its horn erratically, but they didn't bother to look outside and investigate. Why not? Why didn't the person be that nosey neighbor and look out the window? This hurt my heart more than anything. Knowing that had that person just looked out the window, called another neighbor to see what the commotion was, or called the police, Cameron may have had a chance to live.

There were so many questions. Who did Cameron trust to be in his personal space? Being stabbed means that the perpetrator invaded my son's space; whoever did this had to come into close proximity to him and he was unable to defend himself. My son laid on someone's lawn and bled to death. His friends told me that they didn't know who he went to see because he left out the house in basketball shorts, a tank shirt, and slippers. He told them that he would return shortly so there was no reason to ask. Why didn't they just ask who and where? Why didn't Cameron give them more detailed information? I wondered, *Did Cameron mention a name or something while leaving out? Did he know the perpetrator that took his life?*

How many times do people leave the house in something outrageous to go do something really quickly, expecting to be gone for a few minutes? Or when a person intends to pick up or drop off a friend and doesn't plan to get out of the car, so just throws something on? The authorities informed us that Cameron had a rental car that was found in a completely separate location. The car was found burnt, near the Atlanta Zoo. The fire department was dispatched that same night for a car fire, but no one knew that it was the same car that Cameron was driving. The murderer knew exactly how to remove evidence. Cam's body was discarded in a residential neighborhood miles away from where the car he drove was found. His murder was intentional, planned, calculated, and demonic.

More than a year later, Terry and I learned of more damaging information. The coroner's report identified stab wounds covering the front and back of Cameron's body. It was completely graphic in depicting the marks that covered the upper torso, back, and neck. Yet the coroner's poor judgment in keeping the evidence made it almost impossible to find out who murdered my son. It's unbelievable. My son was a victim of a crime and the detectives were told that the coroner's office compromised the investigation because of evidence issues.

Nothing will bring Cameron back to this life, but there is something unsettling about the fact that someone—or whoever was involved with his murder—could take a life and be free to do it again. To know that his murder has not been solved because of the botched trail of evidence and the Georgia Bureau of Investigation's heavy murder caseload is disheartening.

If there was ever a feeling that the world was against me, the way Cameron's case has been handled—yeah, this was it. I kept wondering if something I did caused my son's demise and the aftermath. How would the Georgia Bureau of Investigation ever solve this murder? How could the coroner be so careless and not protect the evidence? As difficult as it was to even think about what really could have happened, something in me wanted Cameron to get the justice anyone should receive on this side of life. I questioned myself over and over again. As a Christian, there was a tendency to think that my wrongdoings had repercussions. There were moments when I repented, hoping that I would never experience the wrath of God. My heart knew the dead end was not about bad luck or generational curses. But knowing that there are expectations and a lifestyle that you live to achieve being an acceptable vessel for God, I could not help but question myself. *Is it me, Oh, Lord?*

It's crazy to be pulled apart in every direction at the same time. That is what it felt like. Yet, I made a choice to trust God amid the devastation and even more so regarding the murder. It might seem crazy, but that's what I did: trusted God. At that juncture, there was nothing else I could do. I had no peace, no hope, and no answers as far as the investigation and justice was concerned. There was also no answers about how I, Cameron's mother, and those who loved him were supposed to accept his sudden death and go on with life without him.

Being blindsided brought out the worst insecurities, doubt, and mistrust. I had no idea what my next steps were, even down to the basics of self-care. Eating, sleeping, and to put it frankly, everything was a chore if I remembered to attend to myself. When the hardship of death hits, it can crush your soul; it can break you into pieces and it feels as if you will never be whole again. The basic functions of life that are taken for granted when life is chipper and fine becomes so hard to do. There were days when I felt as if there was nothing anywhere, at any time, in any way that could bring me comfort. It can be hard to take a breath, to talk, or to drink a glass of water. Everything hurts.

There are many that have had death to come and upset their lives. Whether through physical death, divorce or another failed relationship, or a lost hope or dream, many encounter death and the varied feelings that come with it. Peace is that place where despite the bad, the internal assurance is that it will get better. Well, despite all of the challenges I had to endure beforehand, nothing prepared me for waking up each day in trauma. Nothing prepared me for existing as if there was no peace. When we find ourselves in this place, do we question God? Does our very being beg for answers over and over? For many, yes. Even when some of us feel it is best to "accept what God allows," sometimes we have a dialogue with heaven because we cannot comprehend what we're experiencing to the core of our being. Even then there may be nothing but silence or answers we do not want to hear. And that breeds more questions. *What now? How do you recover and how do you come to grips with a new reality? More importantly, how do you live after death? Where is the forfeited peace that has yet to be obtained?*

The journey that I took was not an overnight success. Not by a long shot, but it was one that I was determined to survive. One thing I knew for sure was that I was not going down without a fight. I had seen close friends grieve until they just about stopped existing as though they had nothing to live for. Life left their eyes and they were taking up space in this world. Grief, despair and maybe even trauma left them changed without the joy of living. Not me. It was not about arrogance, pity or disdain for what I saw in them; it was about recognizing what could happen if I did not fight for the rest of my life because I was so close. Crashing to a point of no return was not an option and there was nowhere else to go but there. I stopped crying not because I was over it, but more so because of the fear of losing my mind and not being able to recover. I did not have any answers. But I was determined. My son may have lost his life, but I wasn't about to lose me.

CHAPTER 7

WHO AM I?

My sorrows have blinded me, keeping the light from shining on my path. Where is the God of my existence and when will He come to rescue the righteous?

Overnight, who I was changed. Death did not ask for permission to enter our lives, and the brokenness did not either. Yet, I imagine my mind did what most do to cling to life, despite grief. Without warning, my thoughts went back and forth from reflecting on the life our family once knew, to the uncertainty and harshness of the present; Instantaneously, I found out that nightmares can last throughout the day. A life without Cameron was my worst nightmare and pervaded every waking moment. The sun could shine, but it was still dark and heavy because my grown adult baby boy was gone. But, I had to figure out how to go on.

The initial few days after finding out posed a problem that could not be solved to my satisfaction. If God delivers us, where was He? Was He going to bring back my beloved son? How could I be rescued from a future without Cameron? While trying to function, my heart clung to the little things. Somehow, it found comfort in reflecting upon Cameron's personality, and the way he had about himself while also questioning what I could have done differently, and may have done wrongly.

Whose shoulder was big enough for me to lean on? My family was going through with me, so how could they carry me? They were deeply affected by Cameron's loss of life in their own ways. Yet I wanted to be rescued. So, I became a ticking time bomb because I shut down all outlets for myself. My emotions were not secure, but I tried my best to manage them, hoping that somehow the pain would subside. I couldn't let that part of me out. The grief that weighted me felt like a huge wool sweater in hundred-degree weather. My soul was heavy and suffocating and I couldn't pull the feeling off of me like the ease of removing a sweater. *How does this work? Would I always feel like this?*

No shower could wash away the pain and signs of depression. The weightiness of grief just stuck to me. My world was so dark that I was afraid to sleep. Sleep? The normal human function became another war zone. I could not control my aversion to it. Anxiety? The onset of insomnia? What was certain was that sleep avoided me and though my brother tried to get me to lie down, it was useless. Too many thoughts were running through my head with the what, how, and when concerning Cameron. The battle was not about me being too afraid to close my eyes for fear of not waking up, but was about the certainty of waking up to an unbearable death in my life. This was the start of a coping mechanism of sleeping with the television on.

Every night, there was a looming sense that the darkness would swallow me up and the light was the fighting agent. I chose a children's station to lull me to sleep every night because the colors were bright in my room and the programming was lighthearted. To be transparent, I slept with the television on for close to five years. It took some time to be able to rest without jumping up in the middle of the night with a panic attack because the bedroom was too dark.

Despite my personal struggles, I was surrounded by my community of believers from the moment the news broke. I barely remember the first few days that followed. Friends and family called, texted, and kept posting condolences on social media. People poured into my home and into my spirit however they could. So many people upheld the family through prayer. I didn't have an ounce of strength left in me and I kept waiting for someone to tell me that this was all a lie. Autopilot is about as close to an emotion I experienced and there was nothing I could do about it. So I sat and stared at blurred faces with muffled voices trying to comfort me. My brother, Joe, took over coordinating everything in the house. I had no clue where DeMaris was, but I did know that some of his friends were there for him. My parents hadn't arrived from Virginia yet but I desperately wanted my mother's hug. There's nothing like needing the touch of the one who God chose to birth you into the world, that of a loving mother. I could no longer be that person to Cameron, but in the cycle of life, my soul yearned for my mother. I wanted someone to make me feel better, but each person I saw had the same expression on their face – helplessness. I knew they had such compassion for me or they wouldn't have shown up. Their hugs were tight and tears were fresh. Others just sat in the corner and silently stared, but I think all of them had the same question in their eyes. *How are you going to get through this Joyce?* Heck if I knew. There were no manuals to this and trying to "fake it to you make it" didn't count. There were no answers. The Olivia Pope-type Jocelyn had no answers, or wisdom to be a fixer. As far as I was concerned this was the first day of hell, and it seemed as if hell was winning.

Hell may be laughing thinking that they have won, but I will be back to fight another day – just not today though. I'm too beat up to lift my hands and stand. I'm a casualty of war called life.

CHAPTER 8

DECISIONS

Lawd, Lord, Lord. There were decisions to be made, and I did not want to make any of them. Cameron died out of state, so there were many phone calls to make concerning transportation arrangements, police reports, the coroner releasing him, and so forth. My family did their best to filter my calls and keep me quiet. The first major decision was that Cameron would be cremated. Our family agreed that no one wanted to see him in a casket. We all wanted to visually remember him alive, laughing and in good spirits.

Cameron had come home to visit in June 2013 during Father's Day. It was a day I cherished the most because the entire family was under one roof. It had been a year since I saw him, so the celebration was two-fold. The last dinner we had was of acceptance and resolution. In the middle of dinner, Cameron stopped eating and just looked at me. I felt that the unspoken conversation was one of him asking and looking for my love. With a loving gaze, I spoke "I love you," and he nodded as if it was all that mattered. He went back to eating and laughing the rest of the evening.

On the last day of the brief visit, he boarded the Megabus in Philly to return to Georgia. I had been so busy that I forgot to get a family picture, so Cameron and DeMaris took one, which is the last memory I have. The sun was setting so they both were squinting; their images looked more like they were angry than simply trying to see me. Cameron kissed DeMaris and said, "Take care of Mommy. I love you, Bentley."

Once again, I heard Cameron call his brother the nickname he gave Demaris because Demaris reminded him of Diddy's, formerly known as Puffy, Puff Daddy, or Puffy Combs' notable umbrella holder, Fonzworth Bentley. Back then, Puffy's assistant was known for being razor sharp, dapper, or casket clean. Although Bentley was an enterprising young man in his own right, being an aide to Diddy made him a Hip Hop celebrity. See, unbeknownst to me, Demaris used to be a helper to residents in our apartment complex and two other neighboring ones. He earned quite a reputation of being a nice young man who would help others, and he earned tips. Cameron's friends teased Demaris about it, although Cameron used to ask Demaris for pizza money or some pocket change from Demaris' good Samaritan earnings. That is how Bentley became Demaris' nickname that rolled off of Cameron's tongue as brotherly banter. Demaris did not seem to mind and maybe because Bentley was impeccably sharp and did menial tasks to advance his career. For Demaris, his goal was simple: keep some money in his pocket. As a boy mom, I learned early on to let my sons navigate most things between themselves, especially things that seemed harmless. Nonetheless, after saying goodbye to Demaris, Cameron hugged me tight, told me he loved me and boarded the bus. That was the last time I saw Cameron alive. That was the last time I saw him face-to-face and felt his loving embrace.

My son had to be cremated. I had no regrets about making that decision for the family. Cameron's spirit left his body more than a week beforehand, and all that was left was a mere shell of him. We did not want to see what was left of him, after he had been murdered. His remains spoke for itself: brutality and suffering. As difficult as it was, Joe and I went to the funeral home to make arrangements to bring Cameron's earthly vessel back home. We pulled up to a funeral home knowing this time it was way too personal. As many times as we had been to funeral homes, this time it is far too close to home. We had to confront morbidity and our care for Cameron was reduced to taking care of his remains. What a feat. Funeral homes are in the business of taking care of the bereaved and giving the deceased a final "resting place." So the stench and atmosphere of death should be expected. But, I hated going there. I hated having to be there. It is one thing to have head knowledge that the family had to deal with Cameron's death. But to have to walk into a place with the stench of death made me cringe. I hated talking to the funeral director to make arrangements for Cameron. As much as the staff tried to be consoling, they were matter-of-factly in their gestures and comments. Of course, that was their job. Nonetheless, everything about being there was unpleasant. By then more than a week had passed and because of the active investigation in Georgia, we had to wait until the police released Cameron's remains to be transported to New Jersey. It was so hard to sit around waiting for Cameron to be released to me. I just wanted him home.

One evening, friends were over and the Coroner called to inform me that she was finished with the autopsy. I wanted to cry all over again because each day of not hearing that he was alive somewhere was killing me. Denial can be ruthless when you're not able to see the evidence or see the evidence and not live in reality. As much as I wanted to deny everything concerning Cameron, the Coroner's call brought me back to my reality. She asked if I wanted a picture, to which I adamantly told her no. No way was I going to view a cold depiction of my son nor was I ready to experience this side of being a murder victim. However, I did ask the Coroner to cut his locs and send them. Cameron knew how to braid hair and at least I could have his hair. The locs had red yarn woven in each strand, a definite standout to the creativity of my son. Cameron wasn't one to blend, but rather to shine and salute life with his own style. Making final arrangements hit home that as much as Cameron loved life, life didn't feel the same way about him.

More decisions had to be made. The family decided to have a memorial service. Since Cameron would be cremated, I wanted that part of letting go to be over because we all had to start this journey of healing. It sounds callous but the truth of the matter is that we just wanted the nightmare to end. At my request, my pastor agreed to speak on the about sovereignty of God. God's sovereignty overrules our desires at times and we may not always understand why. Though I wanted Cameron to still be alive on this earth, the God whom I knew to have wise counsel within Himself didn't need my opinion or thoughts. Believing that this death was for a greater purpose, I trusted God to get me there. I could have argued with God until eternity and still, He would have had the final say. That's what hurt the most – when you earnestly pray and what you get out of it is not what you asked for. However, sometimes when you're at your darkest moments is when God speaks.

The bathroom was the place to cry silently because I didn't want anyone to hear me and chances were that no one would enter without knocking first. One day while hiding away, I sat there thinking that God must be punishing me. How else was this even happening?

Then He spoke. "You can't have it both ways. Either I took him to be with me or left him and hell would have him." Up until that moment, I thought I had felt the sting of death even though I was still alive. God's sovereign voice and words cut like a double-edged sword. It was something I heard, and had to acknowledge.

The Wednesday before Cameron's death, I was in prayer at my church. That night there was such an intensity to pray for Cameron, so I went to a wall and began to pray. "Save Cameron. Don't take him until you save him. Spare his life and make him a vessel for Your Glory." I prayed until I couldn't and didn't leave that wall until I felt a lift that my prayer had reached the throne of God. And yes, one day later he was gone. Never would I have thought that what I wanted through prayer, God's response didn't match it—or did it?

CHAPTER 9

A STRANGER WITHIN

Day whatever: I'm tired, confused, and broken. Days and nights are a blur and the anguish has intensified. My existence is measured by the breaths I take which I count as a reminder that I'm still here.

For those who have lost loved ones, there is a period of waiting that gives us time to avoid the finality of death. For Cameron, that waiting period was a little longer because his body was evidence in a crime that took place in another state. We had to wait for his remains. Two weeks after his death, friends, colleagues, family and loved ones gathered on July 26, 2013, for Cameron Dior Hall's memorial service. We do not get to write the script in life although we get to live out the lines. If Cameron's life were solely up to me, he would have buried his mother, not the other way around.

Large pictures visualized Cameron's life. DeMaris and I led the procession and though I didn't see who was present as I walked down the aisle, I knew they were there. I felt the love and genuine hurt that everyone does not know how to express. Being there made the difference; Demaris and I were not alone. Our tribe was there.

Speaking of tribe, one of my dear friends is a pastor and he gave us the what-in-the-entire-world-did-he-just-do that we did not know we needed. Cameron was gone from this earthly life as we know it. Our family was about to face his mortality in the company of our loved ones, something we were not prepared to do. Nothing can prepare a person how to react, to feel, or to be when it is time to put a loved one to rest. Yet my trusted friend gave us the not-so-appreciated-then shock of our lives during the service. I am not going to call any names, but the letters in his first name are: E, V, E, R, E, T, and T.

Pastor Everett L. Newton, that is his whole government name, was on the program to do the words of comfort. He began with, "Humpty Dumpty sat on a wall. Humpty Dumpty had a great fall…"

Everett recited the entire nursery rhyme. Demaris, with his head bowed, wondered *Did I hear what I just heard?* When Demaris and I staringly looked at the pulpit, the choir behind the dutiful reverend had shoulders jumping up and down; that's how hard they were convulsing and laughing. In real time, I did not think my dear friend was funny. This was supposed to be a moment of comfort, a prayer of comfort. But now, the entire fiasco was lighthearted and hilarious. I do not know what Pastor Newton said after the nursery rhyme because his way of breaking up the heaviness and grief had most of the church laughing. Thank God no one took out their cameras to record, because memes and going viral was not my portion.

The memorial service was a numbing experience knowing that this was the beginning of a new normal. Even when I hoped and prayed that Cameron's death was a hoax, the service brought me back from efforts of denial. My journey to peace did not start when I heard the news, but it started after the final words of comfort were spoken. If there was a time when finality hit hard, that was it. We come from God, and we must return to Him. We may mourn differently, and may not even mourn for long. But the pain of finality of separation is enduring. After the repass and after the last visitor left my house, it was silent. People had returned to their normal routines and mine was shattered. I looked around my house and felt like a stranger. It was hard finding a new norm without wanting to pick up the phone to call Cameron. I just wanted him back in this life.

Loneliness was immediate without a warning. Although Joey, the unofficial manager of the entire situation, and Demaris protected me, my brother and son could not fulfill the emotional voids. I'm single and without a spouse and Cameron's death certainly made me wonder if having a husband would have made a difference. Knowing that there was no one to share my innermost thoughts, pain and tears with was difficult. I had been in a recent relationship, but it was not as meaningful when it came to losing my son because we didn't share a child or the pain. The gentleman had a job, too, and lived quite a distance away. Also, it took me years to realize standing with me must have been quite difficult for him. He had lost his mother, and the timing of my son's tragedy was probably triggering. Sometimes, we may have expectations of people who are not emotionally available because they are treading through their own grief. All I know is the beginning of the aftermath was unbearable. Death made me feel isolated in the world. I was lonely because I had no spouse. I was lonely because my friends had returned to their lives. I was lonely because God wasn't saying anything. Living was a battle in and of itself. Maybe there was nothing to fulfill the emptiness inside. Yet I could have been stranded on an island and would not have felt more alone. There was no fix for losing Cameron. There was no solution that would repair my heart, a mother's heart. My heart wanted to be filled with my son's love and presence or anything that could comfort me.

After the memorial service, just to have one good day took a lot of effort. Battling with my thoughts had a cyclical relationship with my mind, spirit, and mood. One moment I could be fine, then without warning, every breath I took felt as if I were the only person left on earth. At times, I perceived myself as invisible because no one could discern my moments of weakness. All too often those around me would assume that my quietness meant that I was ok, yet my closed mouth was every effort not to scream. Also, sometimes there are just no appropriate words to say. What? What could I express when my heart was broken and my equilibrium was off? The void of losing my son—still with no answers why—played with my emotions. Though my family was around, it was never enough to fill the emptiness. Nothing could.

My heart is hollow yet it beats. My silent voice echoes the pain I cannot express. I've been taken to a place that I desire not to be, yet I must remain until the Light returns.

CHAPTER 10

I AM NOT THE SAME

This unwanted guest refuses to leave my dwelling place. You've been trying to suck the very life out of me and I don't appreciate it. I've asked you to leave on the very first day, and yet you've decided to kick your shoes off and make yourself comfortable.

Grief may be dark, suffocating, and relentless in not letting go, but grief can be conquered. In retrospect, I had to believe this or I would not have made it through. As a Christian, we are taught that although we may face trials, tribulations or testing, we have to go through them. My mind knew this, although what I could not control said otherwise. Along with grief came depression. Many people who are in the stages of grief never understand that depression is present. It transcends normal comprehension—especially when there is no awareness of what grief or depression is. It can feel like trying to see through a thick fog. It can stay longer than we want and will keep rearing its head. The problem is trying to first identify that you are depressed and secondly, navigating through various emotions without damaging yourself and others.

When we are at a loss, we may mourn. It's a normal consequence and in some manner, we have experienced this emotion. No matter how severe your loss is, there will be grief. If I thought that this part of life could be fixed and avoided, I would have been the first to get a pass and pick an easier, more simple emotion to compensate for my loss. I hated grief. I hated what was attributed to me being in it. I hated that I had to endure this process and couldn't figure out how long I would being going through the different stages of grief. When I recall my girlfriend losing her mother, the one thing I paid the most attention to was her grief. I knew she missed her mother, but what I wasn't expecting was the downfall and the uncontrollable spiraling of her life. I witnessed firsthand the changes and felt completely helpless because I couldn't figure out how to help her. When depression started setting in, I could see the physical and emotional transformation like lack of energy, sagging shoulders, constant crying, and the lack of caring for her being. When you are standing on the sidelines looking, there's a true sense of helplessness because unless you have experienced this type of loss, you wouldn't understand the trauma and the emotions. But when Cameron died, I got a firsthand revelation. Within a matter of minutes, I would experience an array of emotions. A sunny day with clouds had me crying uncontrollably. I associated clouds with heaven and my son was there in the clouds. As beautiful as a sunny day could be with its bright clouds against an endless blue background was torture in my eyes. I saw nothing but another day that my son was not with me. How could I be excited for a new day, when all I could think about was what I was missing?

Seeing young men with the same stature as Cameron made me angry. They were living and had nothing to do with Cameron's loss of life, but they served as a reminder that they were still alive and he was not. Smells, sounds, and other similarities triggered emotions that couldn't be controlled. As much as I wanted to turn it off, it came relentlessly in its pursuit without an end in sight. Every day I woke up and there was a test of my emotional waters. *Did I get enough sleep? Was I going to cry today? Do I want to get out of bed?* All of these questions had to be at the forefront of my day if I was going to attempt to have a day without turmoil.

One morning I went to the gym and listened to music on my iPhone. A song from the Walls Group "Make Me Over" came on having no relation to my son, but the lyrics were the cry of my soul: "*I don't wanna live this way again, make me over. Oh Lord, please restore my soul! Make me over again.*" That gut-wrenching moment triggered a panic attack causing me to immediately leave, get in my car and scream all the way home. Only the Lord knew how I got home; I couldn't see through the blinding tears. Those words resonated to the core of my being but one thing I did know, was I wanted someone to fix me. Since I couldn't fix myself with a snap of my finger—from a pep talk, pamper-me moment, or a shopping spree, I needed help to get out of the darkness.

Depression had me believing that my house was safe. Some folks would be okay with that statement, however, when you are grieving, it can become your prison. I would rather lay in the comfort of my bed than get up and move. My room was the only place that didn't require much from me. I could close the door, pull down the shades, and hideaway. It was difficult to go on with everyday life, and seemed easier to remove myself from it. As much as my family was going through the loss of Cameron with me, I didn't even want my family around. Anything that caused me to speak was too much. Even more annoying were questions about what the next steps are. I was knee deep into grief, and still in shock about what was transpiring. There had been a change that I did not anticipate, ask for, or appreciate. One day I realized I am not the same anymore, and will never be.

I had been changed.

Forever.

CHAPTER 11

A Walk in the Dark

With the onset of grief, I felt alone. But the fact is, grief is a universal human experience, a complex and often overwhelming journey that follows the loss of something cherished. Although it is a deeply personal process, many individuals find solace in understanding the stages of grief. If anyone lives long enough, grief will be part of life. I can verify that I went through all the stages of grief first introduced by psychiatrist Elisabeth Kübler-Ross in her groundbreaking 1969 book *On Death and Dying*.

The five stages of grief model provides a framework for comprehending the emotional rollercoaster—and it is a rollercoaster—that accompanies loss. Over time, this model has evolved and expanded to include additional stages and nuances. When we experience loss and grief that comes along with it, understanding the various stages of grief may offer insights into the emotions and challenges that arise during each phase. Whether we realize it or not, most people can identify with the stages of grief. Having been through them, it may be helpful to know how individuals can navigate through them.

1. Denial: The Shield of Protection

The first stage of grief, denial, serves as a protective barrier against the overwhelming reality of loss. It acts as a shock absorber, giving individuals time to process the initial shock and disbelief. During this phase, people might find it difficult to accept the truth, often clinging to hope that the loss isn't permanent. Denial helps individuals to cope with the initial intensity of their emotions, providing a temporary respite.

2. Anger: The Expression of Pain

As the reality of the loss sinks in, denial gives way to anger. Individuals may feel a deep sense of injustice, directing their anger at various targets—the situation, others, themselves, or even a higher power. This stage is a normal and healthy part of the grief process, allowing individuals to channel their pain and frustration into emotional expression. While anger can be intense, acknowledging and understanding its presence can be pivotal in moving forward.

3. Bargaining: The Negotiation of Loss

In an attempt to regain control and reverse the loss, individuals often enter the bargaining stage. This involves seeking compromises or negotiating with a higher power, fate, or even the universe itself. "If only" and "what if" statements become common as people grapple with the idea that they could have done something differently to prevent the loss. Bargaining represents a way for individuals to temporarily soothe their pain by envisioning alternate outcomes.

4. Depression: The Depths of Sorrow

As the initial shock fades, the gravity of the loss becomes more apparent, leading to feelings of profound sadness and emptiness. During this stage, individuals may experience a range of emotions, including loneliness, despair, and helplessness. Depression is a natural response to grief, as it reflects the reality of the situation sinking in. It's important to distinguish between clinical depression and the normal depressive feelings associated with grieving. And if necessary, seek help to cope and deal with the feelings of helplessness.

5. Acceptance: Finding a New Normal

The final stage of grief, acceptance, does not imply forgetting or being unaffected by the loss. Instead, it marks a turning point where individuals begin to understand and come to terms with the new reality. It's important to note that acceptance does not mean approval. It does not mean that a person is in agreement with what has happened. It also does not mean the pain disappears; rather, it signifies the ability to integrate the loss into one's life story and identity. People gradually learn to adapt to the absence and build a new sense of normalcy.

6. Meaning-making: Finding Purpose in Loss

In addition to Kübler-Ross's original five stages, many contemporary models emphasize the importance of finding meaning in grief. This stage involves seeking a sense of purpose or growth from the experience of loss. While not everyone reaches this stage, those who do may discover a renewed perspective on life, a deepened appreciation for relationships, and a drive to honor the memory of what was lost.

7. Reconstruction: Rebuilding a Life

Another modern addition to the stages of grief is the reconstruction phase. This stage acknowledges the ongoing process of rebuilding one's life after the loss. Individuals gradually adjust to their changed circumstances, creating a new identity that includes the absence. The focus shifts from grieving to remembering, healing, and embracing life's new possibilities.

Understanding that grief is not a linear process is crucial. People may move through the stages in different orders or revisit certain stages as they navigate their journey. There's no "right" way to grieve, and everyone's experience is unique. By acknowledging and respecting the stages of grief, individuals can find support, compassion, and healing as they navigate the challenging terrain of loss. This is something I had to learn, because going through the stages of grief and encountering them again made me wonder if I would ever be able to move on. At the time, I did not have a "textbook" awareness of what I was experiencing. But it was frustrating to feel like I made some progress, and in an instant of a second, fell into another period of unbearable grief.

Recently, someone posted on social media the following statement: Grief is sneaky. If this isn't the truth, I don't know what is. Grief sneaks up, without an invitation and unannounced. One minute, I could be at work having a good day. Then, a trigger could pop up without warning; a smell, a phrase that Cameron would use, a smile, or anything that pulled on my motherhood strings could send me into an emotional fit that I could not control. I had to maintain my professionalism while a flood of feelings made me want to explode. The normal Jocelyn thought breaking down was not an option. I had to be introduced to the new me, the one who had no control over how I responded to a panic attack.

A road long forgotten is the road I choose to take. Taking the shortcut may be quicker but not easier. Some things just require a glance in the rear view...

Ever find yourself alone on a road and think you should have stayed on the main highway? It did not take long for me to learn that death and living from the aftermath is a single walk. No one is on the road but you. It does not matter how many persons are experiencing the same journey alongside you, or have before you, when it is your turn, it is something that you have to walk out in your own way.

Interestingly enough, my first attempt to go back to work showed me how vulnerable I was. Thinking that I had been off work long enough, I decided to go back in September to start getting my life back on track. Returning to my office, colleagues and the normal routine was inevitable. I was ready, right? My hopes were up. Boy was I way off.

The first day was rough, knowing my co-workers would want to know how I was feeling. The organization I work for is like family. For those who have long-term working relationships with colleagues, we know what a work family is. When people work together and spend more hours in a workweek than they do with their families, for years, we are bound to get to know one another. It was obvious that my family at work were genuinely concerned. We tend to celebrate a lot of events together—retirements, birthdays, weddings—and are there when someone loses a loved one. So when I returned to work, my work family was pulling for me. They were so excited to see me. Many of them had seen Cameron grow from a young boy to the man he became. When I returned to work, their eyes gave away the curiosity of how I was really doing. As brave as I could be, I smiled and said was fine, knowing I was lying. I didn't trust anyone in the office enough to see my vulnerability; and, even if they noticed I was about to crack, they couldn't fix it. I was that chick in the office—you know the one who has all the answers and can be relied on. Yet I wasn't that superhuman anymore. I was as human as the next person—bruised, battered, and just trying to live again. I could use a hug and cry. That was me. I hated not being strong, but I was just worn out. Did they know how much effort it took just to brush my teeth and put clothes on? Hell no! Did they really want to know how dark things were? Did they really want to be a part of the mess I had in my life? Maybe I robbed myself of support, but I did not think my work family, or any family for that matter, really wanted to know the whole truth. So, I straighten my proverbial tie, plastered a smile on my face and said, "I'm okay."

However, entering my office, I had flashbacks of the day I received the call and almost did not make it. The feeling of hyperventilating could not be suppressed. While on the verge of tears, being at the scene of the pain triggered me. I realized I wasn't ready to wrestle with the emotions that came over me, nor was I prepared to navigate my way through them. It was my first defining moment to overcome the shock and subdue the pain that started this journey. Epic fail. In trying to process through the panic attack, I just closed the door and cried. One of my co-workers was kind enough to go into my office and take down photos of Cameron.

There was one picture perched high on my credenza—Cameron's official high school senior class portrait. He was sixteen years old and his clear caramel complexion was blemish-free. He smiled, no teeth showing to intentionally hide his gapped teeth—a strong paternal trait—and his hair was cut low. He had on a black tuxedo that the school provided. His eyes were clear and his mother was a proud peacock at the moment. I was so proud of my firstborn son and the young man he was becoming. Memories, precious memories. I had persuaded him, to be honest I manipulated him, because I didn't want him to have braids for his high school picture, and told him he could not wear braids and play football at college. It was funny back then, but he was mad at me. By the time he got to Gilford College in Greensboro, North Carolina and realized that there were teammates with long locs, he promised that he would never cut his hair again. It was a vow he kept to the very end. He really didn't like the shape of his head with a pointed crown and flat in the back. I remember rubbing that skull trying to round it because it was so pointy. An old wise tale of rubbing oil to shape a newborn's cranium had some benefits, but didn't fix Cameron's pointy head. That same head shape was definitely passed down from his father, Terry. Cameron worked hard at growing thick medium brown hair and his locs fell past his shoulders. He was the spitting image of his father in every way including the tone of his voice, perception, demeanor and head. Cam just didn't like being identified by his head. So the journey to regrow his hair didn't take long and his braids became part of his identity, look and freedom. He even became a braid specialist making designs for which a lot of people searched him out.

One picture that was formerly a source of motivation and joy, took me down memory lane. At the tender time of just memorializing him, that lane was too painful. I couldn't bring myself to bring down the picture. So yeah, I made up a story about needing to dust. One of my co-workers, who was over six feet tall, reached up and took Cameron's picture down. He gently placed it in my hands. All of a sudden, the portrait in my hands represented pain. What used to be my pride and joy, was a reminder of my present and future state. The image of my son in the picture did not attract a smile anymore like when I used to open the door and see my family. No, it was weighty and the pull had me in a panic. I felt like a coward for not keeping Cam's picture there, but I needed to survive. I placed it in a drawer under some papers. Don't ask me why I did it, I just did. It didn't look right seeing the gap in the family photos, just like it didn't feel right that I had to live without my son. Needless to say, there was no dusting and I spent the remainder of my time doing busy work to keep my mind focused on my professional life and less on my personal life.

My attempt to go back to work didn't last for a week. I asked for more time off without a timeline for returning. Thank God my boss understood. Both of us knew I was nowhere near being okay. The "fake it until you make it" did not work at all with grief. My main dilemma was the trauma, but the new reality was me teetering on a delicate balance to maintain my sanity. For nearly two months I coped and tried to function from day to day before going back to work. Dealing with people was too much. The sympathetic faces with the repeated phrase, "I'm sorry for your loss," wreaked havoc on my psyche. There was no way I could I operate in auto pilot until I figured it out. Employees still came into the office and meetings were still happening, yet the adjustment to a new normal wasn't working. My mistake was thinking I was ready for the world with this new normal. There was no planning on my part in this effort, just a feel-good moment and feeling some boredom got me back into the office. The choice was made for me to take a few more weeks off to get myself in a better mental state; not that I felt defeated, but getting my act together was frustrating. Trying to self-reflect was a place in my mind where I found myself running to, a lot more than usual. Otherwise, much of my thoughts were in survival mode. Just to get to the next hour was a relief.

How long could I stay in the mode where all I did was try to get by, to make it to another day? My life needed more than just getting by but making decisions and changes that would affect the rest of my life. I still had obligations to attend to, a son who still needed me, and parents and a brother who wanted me to be more than alright. As much as I loved Demaris and wanted to live to help him get through this too, I needed to be on a road to recovery and peace. I called my own self out. My life was worth living. God is still on the throne. I was in the midst of every sermon where the preacher closes with, "Hold on, and don't let go. Romans 8:18 declares, 'For I reckon that the sufferings of this present time are not worthy to be compared to the glory which shall be revealed in us.' My brother, my sister, now is not the time to lose hope. Now is not the time to give in! This suffering is but for a moment, but cling to the glory…the future glory that will be revealed."

The family was in the midst of a battle. We were far from Roman armor or the threat of deadly persecution by the government for our public display of our faith. But we were not exempt from the evil that is in this world. Christians love the glory part of our story, but some of that comes with hardship. That is what the fiery trials are all about. One of the most challenging lessons I had to learn was we may have to go from battle to battle and we do not get to change teams because things are hard. There are times when we cannot fight for ourselves, more or less anyone else. During those times, we are assured the Comforter is with us. Even when we are in a strong battle, we have to stay true to who we are in Christ. This conviction and reminder that truly, I was not alone, was as strong as ever. But that does not mean I was not battling insomnia, anxiety, and depression. My faith and hope was alive and well, yet there was a very present struggle. This required really looking and making certain decisions to bring an alignment with my body and spirit. I had to concentrate on being healed emotionally.

Like an open wound, I began to pray and ask God to start my healing process. Giving myself these little pep talks, I made it my daily mantra to speak positive words over my life, to open my mouth and hear myself say: *Your life was made by God. You can make it today. One step equals one victory. It's okay to cry. You'll feel better when it's over.*

As corny as these words may sound to others, they were a small step to getting my mind in the right frame for returning to work, and getting back into the swing of things. Before my son was murdered, there were days when I moaned and complained. But this here was different!

It's an overwhelming feeling to figure out a new normal when you're not ready for it. It takes time and boldness. Everyone wanted to know what happened and it was time-consuming to address them all. Aside from the fact that our family was still without answers surrounding why and who murdered Cameron, approaching the topic was extremely uncomfortable. Knowing that I had choices, made the transition back to work a little easier. Every day wasn't fun-filled, but every day was a chance. That's all that was needed—a chance. Grief eased a bit when you allow yourself to take a chance. If I felt uncomfortable when someone asked about my son, I took the opportunity to tell them it wasn't up for discussion.

Any door that opened for me to pursue peace and to keep my sanity, I walked right through it. Call me selfish, but it was about me, survival and I wasn't going to sabotage any progress I made. My advice to anyone now is don't despise the small things—baby steps will get you there. It just may take some time to get to your desired state.

For me, the flip side was, I had to stay engaged in life. Work was a principal means of doing so. Having to have to do something was an anchor to the outside world, to be useful, to have to communicate with others. I could not check out from my job forever. I had to show up. Working had been key to my routine since I got out of college, and it took Cameron's passing to really bring home how difficult existing through grief and depression can be. The little things, the habitual things, the easy things can become too much when there is no desire, or ability, to function. So grief can be sneaky, and it can be a beast to endure.

CHAPTER 12

PRIORITIES MATTER

Each new day is a day of new mercy. Opening my eyes when it was a struggle to close them made it difficult to breathe without thinking of Cameron and how our family would continue to live without him. It is safe to say, many things were taken for granted before Cameron's murder and that includes waking up in peace and a mind to be grateful for my life, a new day, and a hopeful future. While navigating through the phases of grief, I found myself reflecting upon memories; certain things that may have been unnoticed or nothing special before became a thought to cling to, like a life raft needed during an emergency on a deep lake. It's almost as if I had to cling to these thoughts so I would not let go of Cameron and the life our family had beforehand. One day, one moment, one phone call changed our lives and we had to figure out what that meant. For some reason, reflecting upon my life, where I thought I was in it, my family, our blessings, our progress, and the joy we once had as a unit was something that I had to do. Cameron was gone, but constantly thinking about his life—our lives—was necessary to keep him alive, or at least to keep his memory alive.

Thoughts of my sons centered around how adventurous they were. That is something I attribute to me. Their adventurous spirits come from me. As kids, they were willing to try anything once and not regret doing so. I have this internal bucket list that in my travels I have silently checked off and hope at the same time this isn't the last time I'll experience it. Like going to Costa Rica and trying the zip line over the jungle. At first, I thought we were going on just one line. That turned into eleven and unbeknownst to me each line went higher and longer than the last. At one point I wanted it to stop, but once you start there's no turning back. Lord knows that was one adventure not to be repeated. I was exhausted, and looked around for snakes and jaguars which we were told were very much a part of the tropical landscape. Whew. Everything went well, but traipsing through a hot jungle with wild animals was something I may never repeat. Yet, I am ready to check off other bucket list items like visiting new countries to experience the vast beauty of the world.

When I was younger, I had different priorities, or things that I valued. I used to be more concerned about my beauty. I was a little bit too thick to be skinny and too thin to be chunky. As I've grown into adulthood, my inner beauty thrived and I've found my niche in life. The simplest things bring me joy and plant a genuine smile on my face. My thumbs are green, so to speak. Because I am aspiring to be a home gardener, there are plants all over my home.

Green life creates an environment filled with peace and tranquility. I pride myself when others visit me, because they experience a sense of calm each time they enter. This is ultimately who I am—someone who strives to keep and maintain peace. The older I get, the more I value peace. Remembering the disappointments in life makes me reconsider what is important. I've learned to appreciate myself and others have also. Don't get me wrong. The mistakes that I've made have been costly. Instead of feeling defeated, those times were steppingstones for me to bounce back. Striving, particularly when times are hard, has helped my self-acceptance.

Some think I'm funny, and most would say I'm considerate. One of my perspectives in life is that your journey is what you make it to be. Of course we do not always get to choose what we face in life. But we do get to choose who we are, how we approach what we must face, and our attitude towards facing it.

My family is my life and my anchor. Being a single mother has been a gift. Be, but I cannot address their concerns when my children, and those of other single moms, depend upon us to be their parents. We are the ones they look to for everything in life, while they develop and grow. We provide guidance, care, love, and what they need to live. We may have help from family and friends, and may be blessed to co-parent. However, cherishing every moment and step, being attendant to every scrape, bruise or heartache, finding out what matters to my children, making sure they have what they need, and preparing them for a productive life has been my greatest joy. Despite pressure, disappointment, uncertainty, and unspeakable exhaustion at times, I would not change anything for the world. Motherhood is both challenging and rewarding. I don't call myself Wonder Woman by any means. I am that mom who had the responsibility of ensuring my children had a roof over their heads, clothing, and food. Being a parent is part of who I am. Loving motherhood is within the fabric of my being.

Over time, our immediate family finally had stability, and we were living the dream. We lived in a home I owned and I had become financially stable. Although the reality of parenting had its challenges, we were doing fine. It would be fair to say that I was successful in raising my children. By 2013, both Cameron and DeMaris were out of high school. Cameron lived in Stockbridge, Georgia, while DeMaris attended college locally. The plan was to position myself to leave a legacy for my sons. Not only would they have an inheritance, but if they ever departed from Christianity, they would find their own way and return to the faith they once knew. They were present to witness that in due time, hard work and persistence pays off. Also, with God nothing is impossible.

My life was at a place of peace and contentment. Every accomplishment is because of God's grace. I am a Christian and have been since the age of fourteen. To take back the coopted term "church girl," that is exactly what I am. I am a woman who grew up in church. I love Jesus, going to church, the Word, and to sing. Formidable relationships have been formed from childhood friends from church. I have always been faithful to my local church and active among the community of believers. I grew up in church knowing the promises of God and that the life of Jesus Christ is the bridge that closes the gap between me and the Father. My past and current pastors instilled in me the knowledge and understanding of the Word of God that is the most critical resource and life-changer. I was ready, but did not know it. I was ready because the very Word of God that I did not want to hear, well-wishers offered in attempts to provide genuine consolation. The Word is alive and had already taken hold of me and was working on my behalf. When the Apostle Paul penned Romans 8:35-39, as many times it was quoted, remembered, and preached, I wonder if he knew his divinely inspired words would give me life today. This passage of Scripture has been a viable part of my life while facing one of the darkest moments:

"Who can separate us from the love of Christ? Can affliction, distress or persecution or famine or sword? As it is written: Because of you we are being put to death all day long. No, in all these things we are more than conquerors through him who loved us. For I am persuaded that neither death nor life, nor angels nor rulers, nor things present nor things to come, nor powers, nor height nor depth, nor any other created thing will be able to separate us from the love of God that is in Christ Jesus our Lord" Romans 8:35-39 (CSB).

This is my testimony. Shocked, angry, and in despair, my shattered soul still had an anchor in Jesus. My life, our lives, took a turn that I did not want at all, and did not seek our advice or approval. We had to learn how to live with what we do not like and never wanted to happen. It is God's Word that kept me at my weakest moments. Memories, thoughts, and questions ran through my mind but always encountered God's Word working on my behalf.

CHAPTER 13

I Don't Want to be in This Club

In 2018, I spent a few moments watching television like I normally do. There were news reports and posts all over social media about a shooting in a Kentucky school. Two sixteen-year-olds lost their lives. I wept; my heart was overwhelmed for the parents who were introduced to the pain of finding out their children were murdered. Whew. That is a feeling I know all too well. Before Cameron was taken out of this world, I empathized with such reports. Some would actually stop me in my tracks to the point where I would intercede for the surviving families. It's part of being human. Some things we do not ever want to understand or experience firsthand.

By the time the news of this incident hit the media, I watched mothers stand in the shoes of fresh loss. I listened to them express gratitude through tears. It was just the beginning for them, because the river of tears may never stop. Who wants to join the mothers of children who have been violently killed? This is a part of life that no one ever plans for when children are young and we watch them grow. We observe them in their innocence and hope they will find their place in this world. Their entire future is ahead of them, and when we say that, it means a lifetime, not just a few more days or months due to tragedy. And then something happens that makes us part of a life experience that makes us synergetic.

I am already in a sorority and a tight-knit group of friends and church family. Yet, there is a common bond forged in tragedy between mothers of murdered children and it is not a badge of honor. We may never cross paths personally. But there is a similarity where without warning, we have to figure out how to live knowing not only were our children robbed of their lives and future, but they were taken from us. In 2018, the anguish of watching those tears flow from the mothers' eyes took me back to the anguish of the moment I learned my first born, Cameron, was killed in 2013. Time and time again, I revisit the pain of mourning mothers of children who are violently killed. I could not help but wonder what was going through Cameron's mind during his last few minutes on earth. Most of all, there is an instinct to protect our children. My heart hurts about what my mind already knows. I could not protect my son. Then the final wound is my son's murder became a cold case file; without major attention from social media or special investigative reporting, his case has never been a priority to solve. Although Cameron did not die by racially motivated police brutality, his death is just another young Black man's death amounting to a case number in the system. It's almost as if the family or a grass roots organization does not take extra measures to seek justice, the system will not.

The struggle for justice in the United States has been rife with stories of pain, resilience, and perseverance. Within this larger narrative, the mothers of Black men who have been tragically murdered have emerged as powerful advocates for change, standing at the forefront of the fight against systemic injustice. Through their grief, they have transformed their pain into a potent force for change, their voices echoing through the streets, courtrooms, and hearts of a nation in need of reform. It took quite a bit of time for me to even inquire about what happened to Cameron other than the initial conversations with the Georgia Bureau of Investigation. I just did not have the strength. For years, Terry took the lead in dealing with the detectives.

Meanwhile, the journey of mothers of murdered sons begins with a devastating event that shatters our worlds: the loss of a beloved son. In the face of this unspeakable tragedy, a handful are thrust into the public eye as symbols of grief, rage, and determination. As we grapple with our emotions, we must also navigate the complexities of a justice system that all too often fails to deliver accountability for the perpetrators of these heinous crimes.

For mothers in this tribe, seeking justice isn't just a pursuit of legal retribution—it's a mission to ensure that our sons' lives are not reduced to statistics or footnotes in a larger societal narrative. Our voices become a powerful tool to highlight the systemic issues that led to these deaths and to demand that change take place. Even though our children can no longer speak or advocate for themselves, we can. We can demand that our children are as worthy as everyone else's.

In their quest for justice, these mothers face a daunting array of obstacles. They encounter a legal system that can be slow, biased, and unresponsive to their cries for accountability. If mothers, fathers, family members, advocates and attorney do not hold the local to federal government accountable, the murderers who often have high visibility, will go free. They will be able to inflict the chaos and pain upon other families if they are not stopped. Despite these challenges, mothers prove time and time again that their resolve knows no bounds.

Fueled by a mother's love, they take to the streets, organizing protests, marches, and demonstrations that bring attention to the names and stories of their sons. Through the power of their collective voice, they force the nation to confront uncomfortable truths about racial bias, police brutality, and the urgent need for systemic change. It is not popular, but it is a truth we must confront. Certain persons in our society are often overlooked and not granted the same regard as others. A mother's love lives on, even when our beloved children are gone. Grief and adjusting to the shock of it all is often compounded with action. I did not have the strength to keep pursuing the Georgia Bureau of Investigation.

But I understand how mothers are driven to give their all to address the injustice.

As they transform their grief into action, these mothers become leaders in a movement that transcends individual loss. They stand united, drawing strength from one another's experiences and providing a support network that empowers them to face adversity head-on. They form organizations, advocate for policy changes, and amplify the voices of other marginalized communities affected by similar injustices. Their tireless efforts yield results. Legislative reforms, changes in policies and practices, and increased awareness become the fruits of their labor. In the midst of their personal pain, these mothers find solace in knowing that our sons' lives were not lost in vain.

In the end, the mothers of murdered children in the United States who seek justice for their children become symbols of strength, resilience, and unyielding love. We are all over the country, most are not national news stories or social media viral. Out of the darkest of circumstances, a light can emerge. While the road to justice may be long and arduous, it is a journey that cannot be abandoned until true equality and accountability are achieved.

CHAPTER 14

THE REAL MEANING OF LIFE

A storm is coming. It's dark, looming, raging, and powerful. I can't see it, for I only see the sun shining before me. I'm not prepared to hide and it's gonna take me off guard...

Death.

It's a word that means cessation of life. When death is present, life in this world as we know it, ends. Someday, all of us will experience it. There aren't any words to describe the emotions that are associated with death that depicts the agony and loss felt when we lose a loved one. Movies glorify it as though it's some badge of honor, but the depiction of it doesn't match the tears, grief, or helplessness that those left behind have and fight to live beyond.

Death is so final – no reruns. We can't put life on pause, fix the issue, come back, get it right, make another decision, and try again as if nothing ever happened. Even though we cling onto different beliefs or theories–something, anything to ease the pain–for the most part, accepting the departure and separation of loved ones is difficult. We may even have a fleeting moment when there's consolation that our loved ones are spirits flying around like in the movie *Ghost*. Demi Moore and Patrick Swayze co-star in the movie. She's on the potter's wheel and Patrick comes behind to help her mold the clay. The sense that Demi feels his presence gives the viewer the idea that we feel our loved ones in the afterlife. This doesn't even come close to reality, and I definitely do not believe what Hollywood has depicted. I've come to realize that death is not something we prepare for. It's unexpected, unpredicted and there are no boundaries that it won't cross. Some would say that they were prepared for it—like somehow it would ease the pain. I'm not sure about that and I am no expert, but all I know is that nothing would have prepared me for my experience. I often wonder why God chose me for this time in my life to go through the death of a loved one. I'm not exonerated from it, but I thought that death would come to the older before the younger. Yeah, it's delusional when all television networks daily report of the young dying like an everyday occurrence. How wrong I was to think that God would give me a pass as though I was immune from such a hit.

I was entitled being a Christian living in this world. It should be funny saying it, yet we live thinking that some things should never be a part of our lives. Even though I have gone through a lot as a single mother, I believed that most of the atrocities in this world would not be at my doorstep, especially murder. I'm not even sure if death coming by illness, or accident would be any better, but to murder someone is an evil that tears at the very fabric of your being. As much as you see on the news, social media, and conversations, nothing is more heart-wrenching than to know that someone precious to you was taken away by a dark soul whose assignment from hell was to destroy you, your family, and your faith in God.

Life is sweet and bitter. Sour and tart. The smell can be divine or deceiving.

How can I know the difference when it is placed on my pallet at the same time?

I was well within the cycles of grief without an intellectual knowing of what was happening. Somehow, I kept clinging to memories and rehearsing thoughts that would never lead to a different outcome. If it was for the thousandth time, or the millionth, my heart kept reminiscing about my son. Sometimes those intense revisits to the past made me wonder if I had done things differently, would Cameron have still been alive.

Cameron was a lovable child with a great personality. He was larger than life because his stature made him taller than most in his early years and weight-wise until he reached his late teens. He was chubby as a kid and had me frequently shopping at JCPenney for boys' husky clothing. However, I knew that with his size came the responsibility that he would never be smaller than the other kids his age. A thick waist meant a longer pant length that had to be rolled up to match his height. His foot size—my lord today—was above average and buying good quality footwear meant more money coming out of the pocket. Yet, my tribe matched the assignment ensuring that my baby boy would be clean. Even with the birth of my second son, DeMaris, there was not anything I wouldn't do for my sons.

While Cameron was growing up, there was never a dull moment with him. He played basketball, football and played the saxophone in the school band. He had an animated demeanor that kept me on my feet and laughing, especially when he played the sax. Cameron was in middle school when his father purchased the sax from a pawn shop when Cameron showed an interest in music. The instrument had seen its better days with worn felt pads on the keys and scratches along the bow. But it was new to Cameron; I used to laugh when I thought about how he looked lugging the large saxophone case to school. He was excited and determined to get on the school band he took lessons twice a week after school. After a while, the lessons transferred to home where the squawking and high pitch squeals attacked our eardrums relentlessly until he figured out the correct method of blowing into the reed. Cameron spent many afternoons blowing and trying to make the sax sound peaceful, yet the cracking and squeaking far outweighed the intended goal. But practice makes perfect. Irritations aside, I was proud of all of his accomplishments like a mother should be, and I had more dreams of him being successful than he could have dreamt himself.

Cameron transitioned from an athletic enthusiast to a passion for food. He was always into music, but somehow he became interested in cooking. Any entrée he prepared had some type of spice that was beyond hot. His slogan was "if it doesn't make you sweat, then it's not hot." I envisioned him opening a restaurant named after me and just enjoying his hard work pay off for his future and happiness. I recall one time that I asked him to make spaghetti. Well, I came home to this delightful looking meal only to taste and realize that Cameron had added red pepper flakes in the sauce. My eyes watered and my nose ran like a faucet! He had the audacity to tell me it wasn't hot but I begged to differ because my mouth had a burning sensation that just wouldn't go away.

The figure of speech "jack of all trades, master of none" embodies the thought that when a person does a lot of different things, that person forgoes expertise and does not master any of them. Well, introducing Cameron and all the people who are gifted and have an excellent spirit. There are people who just about anything they touch, they do well. My son may have dibbled and dabbled in one thing and moved onto another. But as he found out where his talents and fulfillment were, he fell in love with art. He was a gifted and loved the music arts. He was into hip-hop and would be in his room all night making music, recording it on his phone and whatever device he could get his hands on. He often told me that by the time he turned thirty, he would become a millionaire. Any and everything without a limit was viable for Cameron. He could be successful at anything if he wanted to, and applied himself. It was just a matter of time and opportunity.

However, on January 1, 2007, things changed. I woke up to a knock on the door to find the police on the other end issuing a warrant for Cameron's arrest. Just days before, his friends called to tell me that Cameron was in the hospital. Thinking the worst, I rushed to the hospital, and he was okay. He sustained cuts and bruises from a fight he'd gotten into. However, one wound was from a screwdriver that pierced his jaw and barely missed his jugular vein. As more information about the altercation unfolded, I knew law enforcement would be involved even though Cameron was defending himself. The error was his friends escorted him away to seek medical attention and because of the severity of the fight, the police were called. As it turned out, Cameron was charged with aggravated assault along with other charges associated with the fight. That one incident put him in prison for three years. It didn't even matter that the individual he was fighting was a convicted felon who was released a few months prior. Even with obtaining a lawyer, Cameron's perceptions of life drastically changed. Instead of him accepting three years of probation, he allowed people to convince him that serving his full time in jail was better.

On March 30, 2010, Cameron was released with one year of probation. It was an unbelievable moment for our family to finally have him home. We were so relieved to have him back with us and couldn't wait for him to return to a normal life. During those three years in prison, I spent those moments praying for reconciliation for my son and everything around him. With all that is rumored about prison life, I prayed for his safety and that he was unharmed while serving his time. He went in at the age of nineteen with a lot of uncertainty and anger from not being able to adjust to life. I remember moments of Cameron trying to fit in with friends and looking for acceptance from them. I believed wholeheartedly that God had spared his life despite the choices he was making, but more importantly because he had a praying mother. Weekly, DeMaris and I visited to encourage him as much as possible. I was even encouraging myself knowing that Cameron was looking for comfort from us when we showed up. Cameron knew that this defining moment in his life required that he get himself back on track and not become caught up in the vicious cycle that could ultimately keep him in the judicial system longer than he wanted to be. I couldn't imagine what it was like being incarcerated—having your freedom stripped, keeping yourself guarded and waiting until time served. It was hard for us all knowing that each time we visited we were not bringing him home, but we kept our promise to return and we did so for three years.

During probation, Cameron obtained a Servsafe certificate at Cathedral Kitchen in Camden, New Jersey. This facility, funded by donations, was instrumental in getting Cameron acclimated back into the workforce. The certification allowed him to handle and prepare food, so that dream I had for him to own a restaurant was on track. I was so excited and wanted him to succeed in life. Once he put his mind to it, in due time Cameron would get back on his feet and pursue life.

Once Cameron relocated to Georgia, he hit the ground running and got a job as a pizza deliveryman in Stockbridge, Georgia. He needed to earn money to make his way, and things were looking up. All of these events had me staying before God in prayer reminding Him of the promises and the prophecies in me and my children's lives. So, yes, with all that was going on I still believed Cameron's setback was not the final say. God is faithful. I reminded myself that Cameron had a heritage full of good and through prayer and being faithful, God would restore Cameron. All that I read in the Bible, heard in sermons and motivational speeches inspired me to believe. All I needed to do was get through this temporary setback. We've all had those in life and a little bump in the road doesn't stop the new momentum we have going for us. Life was a little bitter, but with some time, steadfastness in prayer, and expectation, it would return to being sweet again. Things had to get better.

So yeah, I was depressed. My hopes died when Cameron did and I could not understand why. *Why is it so difficult to take up the broken pieces and move on?* Time and time again, my thoughts veered into the past. My heart was shattered, and I kept replaying in my head all the things I said, didn't say, what he must have thought in his last moments, and the list went on. The thought of him dying alone tore me up inside. That part of grief and depression had me close to asking my family to admit me into a mental ward. When someone has uncontrolled thoughts that recycle during the grief process, it can become dangerous if they are not expressed to someone who can assist in getting help, and if need be. Accountability is necessary. Grown men have wept and taken their own lives behind the intensity of grief and depression. Many who have endured will tell you that it's a life-altering experience. It's a change to your existence.

Second guessing myself was crippling me. Was it insecurity? Anxiety? What was I even doing because from my standpoint, I didn't think I was doing a good job at whatever this life was asking of me. It felt like the rug was pulled from under my feet and I came crashing down and Cameron was gone forever. There was no way that my life full of pain could result in something good. How could it be when the struggle of just breathing and getting out of bed was a daunting task? Regardless, I plastered a smile on my face in front of my family and friends. I was suffering and wanted to be alright. All of us fixed our faces in order to let one another think we were not as wounded and broken as we were. Our quiet moments could have been crying sessions, but we never let on. Just when I thought battling depression, anxiety, bouts of insomnia, and fluttering back and forth through grief was going to be a new norm, something happened. A turnaround came—right on time!

CHAPTER 15

THE BREAKING

One Friday night, I traveled to church and my mood changed. It was so heavy and dark, a feeling that I had never experienced before. Mentally, it was very dark. There was no suicidal ideation. Nope, that was not it. But there was a sense that I would never be right or genuinely happy again. I physically showed up to the church, but mentally struggled with how I was going to get this feeling off me. Before the service ended, I confessed my depression and asked for prayer. It was a desperate attempt to get God's attention and ask for help. My pastor at the time, Prophet Mathias Guerard, along with church members earnestly prayed for God to remove the depression and to keep my mind at peace. Their relentless pursuit of prayer gave me the relief and clarity needed to get through the night though I still had a long journey ahead of me. That is the moment when I felt that I could breathe again. So I inhaled.

Freedom from depression gave me enough energy to move. The weight I had been carrying kept me in a state of immobility. Just imagine waking up every morning and trying to lift your head off the pillow. Throughout the day, movement was down to the bare minimum because there was no need to do anything beyond just breathing. Looking back, psychological and physical activity were necessary for healing. The struggle to overcome grief and depression was real. Thoughts of success, peace, and a sense of normalcy didn't exist. Depression worked against my mind that used to cradle inspiring thoughts. What I did not want to do is rationalize and self-diagnose untreated depression. In real time, I reflected on how others had gone through depression and the toll it took on their lives. It was obvious that being in this state could affect my life as well as my family. Recognizing that you're in the mud is one thing, but spinning in it and not concluding that it's getting you nowhere is different. I did not want to keep spinning in the mud. Until I came to terms with my position, then help was elusive. The question of getting out of the mud wasn't as crucial needing to know why I was in it. Breakthrough was manifesting. Wanting to live again—not merely exist, but to live—after Cameron's death was the first constructive step in my journey for peace.

Sometimes, we learn lessons that we do not like. It would have been much easier for God to just whisper some things into my ear, rather than having to learn some things firsthand. That battle to fight for what was left of me, to thrive again, to want to enjoy life again, was a hard one. I didn't want to sit at the window and stare out wishing the day could be better. I needed to be accountable for making the day better by being a part of the day. Days were passing quickly and others had returned to their routine and no matter how painful this season was for my life, I had to be more than death. I was still a living, breathing testament of life with an identity, a name, and made in the image of God. Although depression tried to choke out my existence as a God-fearing, God-praising person, it could not. See, depression cannot be categorized by one single event, nor is it a quick resolve in some cases. Therapy, medication, prayer, talking with friends or looking up articles on the subject may move you further along in the journey for freedom. The journey may not be predictable, either.

Without anything left to lose, I was headed in the right direction. During this time, I experienced triggers. A huge part of my recovery was learning to live despite them. Those reflective occurrences cause moments of discomfort or pain. Triggers have no particular time or reason, but they are quick, sharp, and a reminder of the loss.

The human mind is an intricate web of thoughts, emotions, and reactions, often influenced by a multitude of factors. Among these factors, psychological triggers play a pivotal role in shaping our emotional responses and behaviors. Understanding psychological triggers help to deal with them; at least that is what has happened for me, over time. I did not always have a "knowing" of what was happening. But after reading some materials, it all started to make sense.

Psychological triggers are stimuli that elicit strong emotional or behavioral responses due to their association with past experiences, memories, or traumas. These triggers can be external, such as sights, sounds, or situations, or they can be internal, arising from thoughts, feelings, or bodily sensations. Triggers are deeply personal and often tied to one's unique life experiences and emotional history.

Triggers can evoke a range of emotions, from joy and nostalgia to fear and distress. They operate on an unconscious level, often catching individuals off guard and leading to intense emotional reactions. It's crucial to differentiate between normal emotional responses and triggered reactions. A triggered response is characterized by its intensity, rapid onset, and the feeling of being overwhelmed by emotions.

Aha. This is why walking back into my office at work immediately after Cameron's death led to a panic attack. Losing a loved one to murder is a profoundly traumatic experience that shatters the very foundation of a family. The surviving members find themselves grappling not only with the loss itself but also with the sudden and violent nature of the death. In this context, psychological triggers can become particularly potent, intensifying the grieving process and affecting the overall well-being of the surviving family. There were several instances of re-traumatization where triggers reawakened the trauma of my son's murder, thrusting me and other surviving family members back into the moment of the loss. A particular scent, a news headline, or a location associated with the crime can flood minds with vivid and distressing memories, making it challenging to escape the grasp of the trauma. Even though the details are always different, every time a school shooting, mass murder, or another person is murdered, just scrolling through social media or watching the news can take me right back to the place I was in my whole soul when I was notified of Cameron's murder. Watching other family members—even family allies or local officials—get teary eyed over another senseless loss of life can be triggering.

Triggers can send survivors on an emotional rollercoaster. They might experience sudden bouts of anger, fear, anxiety, or even dissociation when confronted with something reminiscent of the murder or the event that causes association. This can lead to a sense of powerlessness as they struggle to control these intense emotions. For me, just about every July is the time I have to brace myself. Cameron was born in July, and taken from us in July. That is a month when I have to do whatever I can to get through it. All the years of planning and celebrating his birthday turned into an emptiness. But I cannot avoid July. Triggers may cause other responses like isolation and avoidance.

Even without an official decision, sometimes there are things that I, like other survivors, avoid. Survivors might start avoiding places, people, or situations that remind them of the situation, inadvertently isolating themselves from certain aspects of their own lives. While avoidance provides a temporary respite, it can hinder the healing process and prevent processing grief in a healthy manner. This, I experienced firsthand.

Cameron was murdered in the state of Georgia, in a suburb close to the town he lived in. What the detectives have been able to piece together is, the attack took place in the neighborhood where he lived, and Cameron was still alive. He was put into the car he was renting, taken to another city about 25 minutes away, and left in a residential cul-de-sac to die. Then, the car he was using was taken to the far end of that same city and set aflame. According to the evidence, there were at least 3 locations associated with his murder. Like clockwork, after Cameron's passing, I no longer wanted to go anywhere near Atlanta, Georgia, the "ATL" and its outskirts. No! As natural as it is to associate an apple pie, red, white and blue, or the NBA with the United States of America, all of a sudden anywhere in the ATL geographic region became associated with darkness, the place of Cameron's demise. Atlanta is the place where the local authorities rack up dead case files for young men just like my son, because according to them, they are always busy solving murder cases. Years passed before I was able to visit that area, and when I did, it was to be there for a friend who just lost a close relative. The visit was triggering because I did not put two and two together and realize she lives in the same suburban city where Cameron was left to die.

Triggers can also cause relationship strain. Psychological triggers can strain relationships within the surviving family and with others around them. Misunderstandings can arise when triggered reactions are misinterpreted as personal attacks, leading to strained communication and further isolation. Sometimes people do not know what to say, what to do, and they may say the "wrong" thing. What is deemed wrong is totally subjective. For a survivor who does not want to hear Jesus paid it all, the loved one is in a better place now, or at least their troubles are finally over, words of comfort may hit like words of shut up, please. There is no formula. There may even be situations where—and this seems to be a trend of dismissiveness, insensitivity and apathy—people get tired of waiting for their friends and loved ones to be normal again. Or, to get delivered. Or, to stop being a victim. Some may even express concern like, "Shouldn't you be past this by now? How long are you going to mourn?" To be honest, relationships may change. They may see an end or never be the same. Coping with triggers when in the thick of being grief-stricken warrants a conscientiousness and consideration of others the bereaved just may not be able to give. Through my own journey of healing, the need for self-preservation became paramount. I was not always self-aware, or even able to focus on others as I normally would have. Navigating the landscape of psychological triggers is a challenging endeavor, but there are strategies that can help surviving families cope and heal.

1. **Awareness:** Recognizing triggers is the first step to managing them. By identifying personal triggers, survivors can prepare themselves for potential reactions and develop healthy coping mechanisms. This was a healthy outcome

from the trial-and-error process of grieving. It took my son's death for me to prioritize my sanity and well-being. Although triggers can arise from the least expected thing, those that I am aware of are the ones I make decisions to avoid, or at least manage my emotions.

2. **Professional Support:** Seeking therapy or counseling is crucial for survivors to process grief and learn effective coping strategies. Therapists can provide tools to manage triggered responses and guide them towards healing. In my journey, I was not inclined to seek therapy. Looking back, there is not a reason for this decision, maybe it was avoidance. Maybe I was not ready to face any consistent "help" that required me to touch the part of me that could stifle the very breath from my body. Perhaps I was not ready.

3. **Open Communication:** Encouraging open communication within the family allows members to share their triggers and support each other. This fosters understanding and helps family members navigate triggers together.

4. **Self-Care:** Engaging in self-care practices, such as exercise, mindfulness, and creative outlets, can provide a positive outlet for managing triggered emotions and promoting overall well-being.

5. **Gradual Exposure:** With professional guidance, survivors can gradually expose themselves to triggers in a controlled manner, desensitizing their emotional reactions over time.

Psychological triggers have the power to stir up intense emotions and reactions within us, often leading to profound changes in our thoughts and behaviors. For surviving families of murder victims or those who have experienced tragedy, triggers can serve as poignant reminders of their trauma, making the grieving process more intricate and challenging. However, with time, support, and a proactive approach to healing, survivors can learn to manage triggers and find ways to move forward while honoring the memories of their loved ones.

My triggers were pictures of Cameron. I took down every picture in my house, put up all of the photo albums, and hid behind my grief. Though my family silently questioned the move, I had to do it. I'm not sure that anyone walking into my house would have noticed that Cameron's pictures were not visible. My brother Joe, who was staying with me at the time, kept a picture of Cam in his room. Each time I had to go in there, I would avoid eyeing the picture. My heart couldn't take it. Joey even had Cameron's picture as a screen saver on his phone. My mom, who had taken care of Cameron since the day he was born, had pictures all over her house. Not me. His pictures had to be put up and stored which denoted that I was nowhere close to being at peace. We all had to deal with things the way we needed to, and while they wanted constant visual reminders through pictures, that is exactly what I did not want. What kind of a mom was I, who could not, did not want to see pictures of my deceased son? I was a grieving mom who had to live.

The last time Cameron left our New Jersey home, he left a pair of his shoes near the stairway with the intent of returning. Now a small table replaces that spot. No one can leave shoes at the bottom of the steps anymore. There is no rhyme or reason other than what may seem senseless to others, makes total sense for my sanity. I went into safe mode to protect my sanity which when I think about it, didn't do much for it. All I was doing was prolonging the inevitable, which by my standards could be an eternity.

Who will save me from me, a place I cannot see? Who is brave to go beyond my broken and bleeding heart to see the good in me? For I desire to see the goodness of the day, to be free from the bondage within. For who will risk it all for me to see me free from me?

My thoughts ran amuck with all of the "whys" you could imagine. The pain was so great that on most days, all I wanted to do was scream. Since the day of the murder, I still did not have answers from the Georgia Bureau of Investigation (GBI) about the killer, or those who may have been involved. The GBI was no closer to resolving this crime. I had asked Cameron's father Terry to take over in getting answers because, in all honesty, my heart could take it. My fear has been going into a sunken place where my mind "snaps." Yet our family still wanted answers. Who wanted my son dead? Why would someone kill him?

Cameron was a fierce friend to those who knew him and there was nothing that he wouldn't do to help you either. After Terry spoke with the detective, it turns out there was a side of Cameron that we didn't know about. On several occasions, Terry had to correct the lead detective because the investigators used language in their communication that portrayed our son lived a dark life, as though he had no home upbringing. What do you do when you get damaging information like that? Well, I got mad. I was mad that Cameron subjected himself to living well below the standards in which he was raised. It made me angry that in the few months before his death, he was almost a scavenger trying to get a few dollars here and there as though his family in New Jersey and Tennessee couldn't afford to help him out. I worked for the government for more than 30 years and his father was a business owner and worked for a public utility for more than 20 years. So how in the world did our child go from having what he needed to trying to make a dime? These were the questions that gutted me to no end when the person needed to question was no longer around. So, I was left with creating imaginary scenarios to rationalize why Cameron evolved into this person who did things I never knew about.

To make matters worse, guilt reared its head by telling me that I was an inadequate mother. I questioned every decision I made wondering if I did the right thing. Something so trivial like saying "no" when Cameron asked to go to the movies when he was 15, became even bigger once he wasn't here. The list started growing and the thoughts wouldn't stop. What I did for my child—at least as far as my perspective—became weighted. My confidence in the kind of mother I had been became unbearable. This is when I became tormented.

Tormenting spirits are on a mission. They can operate through never-ending, devastating conversations that seem to be on repeat in your head. The thoughts are relentless. Over, and over, and over again, thoughts become torturous. The thoughts can break down your resilience and confidence leaving you to feel helpless and useless.

The last conversation I had with Cameron was him asking for money. I recall telling him that I would do it, but also chastising him about being a better steward of it. After ending the call, I said to my friend, "I know Cameron wants more than what he asked. Why doesn't he just ask? I know I can be harsh, but he knows I will give it to him anyway."

That conversation with Cameron played over and over, like a song on repeat. Each time I dissected it to find any clues about his death. Each time I envisioned our discourse was more tormenting than the last and every time I blamed myself. Apparently, I didn't do enough. Somehow, I had let him down as a mother by not telling him it was okay, and that whatever problems he had that I and his family would fix it. But it didn't get fixed and I never said any of this to him. All of these thoughts along with the derogatory comments from the detective had me mentally jacked up. As much as I wanted to turn my mind off, the eternal rehearsal of what I probably did wrong just seemed to be endless. Was I was losing my mind? What else could it be when I could not shut my thoughts down?

It wasn't until I received a call from my pastor's wife that I was freed from the torment. She called to tell me that she was praying for me and the Spirit of God spoke to her to tell me that I was a good mother. I wept openly as I felt a sense of relief come over me! The very thing that plagued my mind was the very thing she called to address. You just don't know how someone being obedient to God is effective in delivering a life-altering word! My pastor's wife brought the good news, a message of comfort. God loved me enough to tell me that I was a good mother and I was relieved! Thank you, Jesus!

CHAPTER 16

Ugly Firsts

Firsts may be good for some, they used to be great for me. Now, I dread them. I wish I were last in this pain that refuses to release me.

Every moment since Cameron Dior's passing became a "first" experience for me. His birthday, Mother's Day, Father's Day, Spring, Summer—all opened the scab that was trying to heal over my heart. I felt that each time I would have an okay day, a new first would pop up. The first day I managed to sleep and opened up my eyes to a new day and instantly realized my son was gone, was a first to living in this world without my firstborn. For the first few years, breaking the habit of picking up the phone to share something with him, or expecting him to call or come home to visit was hurtful.

By the time July 2014 came, I was having panic attacks. That was the first time an anniversary of his death came around, and I did not want to deal with it. From the 1st through the 31st I was emotional and withdrawn. On the 12th, I tried not to think at all so I could exist without falling apart. I looked at the calendar to check off the days until August 1st when I knew that I had gone through another year. Upon reflection, I'm kind of relieved that all that the most difficult days are within the same month. I'm not saying that it makes it better, but that I don't have to prepare myself for another anniversary of some sort. Those yearly panic attacks lasted three years. Not even my family knew anything about them.

See, Cameron died two weeks before his birthday, all occurring in the month of July. Years of looking forward to July 31st to celebrate him, and to celebrate with him, turned into negative anticipation. Our family was celebration-less since the main birthday celebrant was deceased. Thank God someone made a suggestion to turn this thing back around to a celebration. Our family made a commitment to always remember Cameron and his birthday with the release of balloons. On that day, the skies were clear and about a dozen of us went to the park to release the balloons. I had also called his father and told him what we were doing, so families in Michigan, Texas, Mississippi, and Tennessee gathered together on Cameron's birthday to celebrate our beloved.

It was a beautiful sight to see when the colorful balloons lit up the sky. As they floated in the air, they responded to the difference in the air's density and appeared to be dancing and quickly ascending to heaven. I could only have imagined that Cameron was smiling and laughing at the gesture of love. Also, my goddaughter and Cameron share the same birthday. It made the moment lighter to celebrate her knowing that she had a special bond with Cameron. They would call each other twins although they were five years apart. After releasing the balloons, we decided to celebrate my wonderful goddaughter. She is still alive and making her day special made Cameron's loss more bearable for me. This celebration has become a tradition, and our tight-knit family has not grown weary of remembering Cameron on his birthday. He will never be forgotten.

Getting through the month of July initially was a "whew" moment. However, it was just a reprieve. Seemingly, I was back to square one when the holidays rolled around. Seeing the fall leaves, the weather turn, and holiday advertisements everywhere brought on a familiar anxiety. Facing the holidays without Cameron reversed any grounds I had in the grieving process. Thanksgiving, and especially Christmas, I cried most of the day. Just knowing this would be the way of life going forward was numbing. I wanted to sleep the days away hoping that somehow, I would wake up in another era or another reality. I didn't want to participate in the festivities and by the time New Year's Eve came, I was a mess. The meaning of holidays were slighted through the framework of grief. It made me realize that living this life can make anyone take life for granted. It is easy to automatically expect people to be around forever.

When the hour had come for the new year, I made a decision. I had to leave Cameron in the old. He would forever be in 2013 signaling the end of an era. Everything going forward was memories and those memories were only as good as what our family could remember and what memorabilia we had. Naturally, it became important to preserve all that I had of Cameron. Moving forward, we had to adjust to living without him in our day-to-day lives. Things changed, and we had to change.

The first of anything traumatic is hard. It's a daunting task of trying not to remember but knowing that there isn't another choice but to experience it. My body remembers and reminds me. Trauma works like that. Oftentimes we spend more time and energy trying to avoid what has happened to millions and generations of people throughout the world throughout time. We are human. Those moments are painful reflections of the changes in life that reminds us all that we're not excluded from death, mourning, grief, pain, trauma or tragedy. Death is inevitable. How death happens determines the pain level we all have to endure. Being a victim of murder is one of the most excruciating events that a person can experience. Survivors of murder victims endure unimaginable pain as well. To know that something so horrific happened to a loved one by someone so dark is devastating. Some questions are never answered. Regardless of whether the perpetrator is caught and justice is served doesn't bring those left behind true justice. Our loved ones cannot be replaced. If there's closure at all, it is found in knowing some things are beyond our control. With a life surrendered to Christ— where Jesus is the center of it all—even when we do not understand and resolve is impossible, there is an assurance. The

Lord of all knows. He will draw us out a cycle of endless questions and despair and lead us to a place of peace. As much as we may think we need answers, the more we rely upon God for true healing, we will find that we may have been coddling the wrong questions. Grappling with letting go of uncertainty and a complete report of what happened, made room for peace. I don't know what my son endured before his final breath in this life but am assured that his repentant heart was received by God. I can't imagine the fear of knowing death was near or the cries he made hoping someone would help. But I can rest in believing that God heard his cries of repentance and moved him from earth to glory. And the struggle of death through this dark time of my son's life was changed when he heard the Father's voice to come, and be free from the cares of this life and world. Cameron knew the way of the Lord, and his life has always been in God's hands. God's Word is truth!

> *"Do not be afraid of those who kill the body but cannot kill the soul. Rather, be afraid of the One who can destroy both soul and body in hell"* (Matthew 10:28, New International Version).

If there is any consolation in death, it is in knowing that when a flawed or evil human being murders another, the act may kill the body. But for the redeemed of the Lord, the murderous act cannot kill the soul.

CHAPTER 17

IT'S ANGER AND IT'S OKAY

"Grief is the price we pay for love." – Queen Elizabeth II

Grief looks different for people. Countless grieved when 9/11 occurred. For those of us who lived right in the vicinity of the deadliest terror attacks against the United States of America, the chaos and tragedy was more tangible. Not only did many people know of victims, but the residue of the destruction was visible in the skies. Washington, D.C., Pennsylvania and New York were targeted, and the aftermath of it all became a worldwide moment of grief. September 11, 2001, showed us the vulnerability of our world being turned upside down, without personal warning, and being in danger. It showed us that with all of our strength, efforts and power, we are all vulnerable. It took such an occurrence to shut down the airways over the United States and to cause the world to pause and mourn with us. The media around the world covered the terrorist attack and for months afterwards, shared the stories of those who lost their lives and survivors who ran in fear and fled the scenes for safety. We talked about it, we prayed, and we may have even felt like we wish we would have met some of the victims as we got to know them through their memories and the accounts of their loved ones and coworkers. Humanity stretched its arms wide enough to show that there is nothing like genuine love where strangers risk their lives, donate, and galvanize aid.

Elizabeth II, The late Queen of England, coined a phrase that provided comfort and insight. At the time she addressed the public, the words were impactful. They provided hope so that while so many were grieving, we could hold onto the reason why grief runs so deeply. Her expression is ever so meaningful, especially when grief hits so close to home. If the depth of my love for my sons could be measured, it would explain the depth of the grief I have felt in losing one of them. Her words in part, "Grief is the price we pay for love," will never leave me. They certainly ring true.

Grief can cause a range of emotions. From the onset of the loss and for quite some time afterwards, another emotion experienced was abandonment. No one knows the internal sufferings of those who are grieving. It's so easy to assume that all is well just by looking at the physical. We smile from time to time, but often it's done so that the spectator won't ask questions. Cameron leaving through death left me and DeMaris with feelings of abandonment. We used to be the three amigos and we believed that we would always be together. I can assure you that DeMaris felt the same. His older brother, whom he adored, who also loved him, was taken from him.

Once Cameron was memorialized and the service was over, and everyone returned to their normal life, I was left standing trying to figure out mine. As long as there was activity in the house there was a buffer to shield be from being alone. Once the house got quiet, I didn't want to be left alone. I was in a relationship at the time, and my companion was not around as much. Everybody had to get back to work and since I had developed abandonment issues, I grew anxious about what was happening with my loved ones when they were out of my sight, especially DeMaris. My issues latched onto my him to the point where I was scared for him to leave the house. My fears of him not returning home from school, work, or being out with his friends, amplified. One night I woke up and realized he wasn't home. It was 2 AM and he told me he would be home by 1 AM. I called and texted his phone. No answer. My poor son. I tried to be rational, but my fears won. I panicked and thought the worst. I called his phone over thirty times in the span of two minutes. When he did call back, I went ballistic! I was screaming and crying on the phone because he did promise he would be home by 1 AM. By the time DeMaris did get home, he sat outside and messaged me. He apologized for scaring me, and told me that his phone had died. I did apologize, but it didn't ease the feeling that something could happen to him and I would have no one.

Being left behind and feeling left behind are two different things, although it may feel the same. When others move on with their lives, they may not understand how a withdrawal of constant communication, love and support can come across differently that what it actually is. Emotions stemming from grief can project as such. The reality of funeral services being over and little to no efforts for visits is a starting point. It's the start of navigating through all sorts of emotions and feelings, but getting used to the lack of a person's physical presence. As quickly as people flood to show support it is the same when they go back to their normal routines. The grieved are left to their thoughts and issues without physical support from the outside. Abandonment or separation from anyone who is endeared can't be looked upon as just another person. No, those who are absent from this world have left gaping holes in our lives—permanently. Again, I had questions. *Who can we find comfort when it feels like the rug has been pulled from underneath your feet? Will I be able to get up, stand up, and move forward with life without my son?*

Let's not forget the anger. I spent months being angry at God. The obvious is Cameron, but that was just the snippet of all of the things that were troubling. During my grieving, a few things happened: One friend lost her mom from a long illness shortly after the funeral. My Aunt Virginia died unexpectedly weeks after and, my best friend's nephew was killed almost a month after Cameron's death. All of this happened within a span of one month. I was angry. Couldn't God just give me a break? Could their lives have been spared while I went through my grief? Where is the fairness in all this? How much of a friend and help could I be to others when I was still bleeding?

The anger led to me revisiting every contentious moment in my life and blaming God for everything. It angered me that I was being subjected to additional pain by watching more of my loved ones go through what I was in the midst of my own pain. When was God going to stop? Was He just that cruel? My anger was fueled by not only experiencing this moment, but that there was still no resolution as to who did this to Cameron. God had all the answers and yet no one was speaking. Yes, I blamed God. I blamed Him for not preventing Cameron's death just like I did when my extended family lost their loved ones. Staying mad didn't fix anything, it only hindered progress. Instead of moving forward, I concentrated on all of the things I was denied. There was a list: no marriage, son's life was brutally taken, overlooked promotions, things that happened in my childhood, and the list was never-ending. Yet in that, God remained silent. I guess He figured I was this temper tantrum adult who just wanted to have her way, so He let me vent. I went through the month of August mad at life. Nothing could satisfy me and when my relationship started falling apart, I really gave God an ear full. However, when the dust settled, it became clear that God was really there.

As much as I wanted the pain to stop, I never reverted to other methods like alcohol and drugs. My internal prevention help came from the Helper, the Holy Spirit. He kicked in and reminded me that addiction is real and just because life isn't fair right now doesn't mean it can't be fair. I wasn't the only one that had a tragedy and was suffering. As long as I had life, this death wouldn't be my last rodeo either.

Being transparent, I can admit to being angry at Cameron. As much as I wanted to look in the sky and rant at the one perceived to have been in heaven, there weren't any answers are there. I could have stood over the gravesite and shouted, spit, hollered and screamed. Still, the dead will not respond. You can imagine a conversation or see it in a dream, but there are things that will never be answered in this life. I had to come to those conclusions because knowing that my son's death was criminal, I had to trust God that in time, justice would prevail for me and my family.

After you, there is only me standing in need of whatever will make me whole again.

What's left of me – can it be fixed? Only the Lord knows.

CHAPTER 18

Pivotal Change

I have a decision to make.

I don't know where the edge of darkness lies, but I have to try and find it.

Though darkness covers me, the remnant of my soul speaks – PEACE! PEACE!

The time came to pivot. I was tired: Worn out from the repeated emotions that kept playing with no end in sight. When you're sick and tired of being sick and tired, something has to change. One day, I had enough of myself. There was no way that I wanted to live in this state of grief. I knew that a decision had to be made for my own future. Did I want to stay in this grief or did I want to live? How times have we found ourselves in this position where days and weeks turn into months and maybe even years without any relief? Trials and testing made me see my true character. It happens to all of us. Our faith may be greatly impacted, too. When we've had just about enough of being in this state, like it or not, we have to make decisions.

For every sunrise and sunset since my son's death, I struggled to have moments without crying or being sad about my life. Every. Single. Day. Prior to July 12th, 2013, all was well. Prior to that earmarked date, I thought that I was living my best life, looking forward to retirement, grandchildren, and reflecting on my accomplishments. I wanted to be in that space where my life seemed good and at peace. I'm not talking about Cameron at this moment, but where I as a whole person was and where I could be. There had to be a state of contentment with life in spite of losing a child. Death had disrupted any semblance of normalcy and brought life's momentum to a temporary standstill. In this, the peace which I had known it to be was hijacked during my grief and I wanted it back. Did this tragedy mean that I could no longer have peace in my life? If peace was a person, somehow, I had to reintroduce myself to Peace. I had to find a way to speak to it, court it if necessary, and ask that it be returned to me. I had no idea if I knew what it really was and even questioned my own interpretation. And, I knew I couldn't keep living without it.

There was no way to restart where I had stopped, because of the state I was in, mentally. But I was ready to take steps—baby steps. I had no idea how, but in order for me to get back on my feet, I had to change my mindset about how I viewed my son's death and life without him. With no answers from the Georgia Bureau of Investigations, I was still crippled because my son's murder was not solved. Knowing that his killer could still be out there made me angry. If the person who killed Cameron has not been caught, died, or by some miracle turned their life around, that person could end up causing another family unbearable pain. Even though the situation had not changed, I had to keep changing, because it did change me. There was an overwhelming pain within and I ached to be released from it. Who I am wasn't who I became in tragedy. So peace had to be birthed from the place of tragedy. It had to reach far beyond any place I could have imagined and it definitely had to be an anchor. Knowing that a newfound place of darkness had clouded my perception of life, peace in my mind had to be bigger and stronger than the residuals of death. Changing my mindset became paramount in reclaiming my position in life. When you think that everything has been placed in a holding pattern, at some time you're either going to land the plane or keep circling praying that you don't run out of fuel. What was peace? As simple as the question is, it required reflection on my understanding and what peace is.

When I was a young church girl and "got saved," what other Christians refer to as being born again, something happened. Without "knowing" intellectually or being able to interpret the Scriptures, my whole life changed. I had the Roman 5:1 (NIV) peace with God through Jesus Christ: "Therefore, since we have been justified through faith, we have peace with God through our Lord Jesus Christ." This verse highlights the idea that faith in Jesus Christ leads to reconciliation and peace with God. As I grew older and became more committed to my faith, I understood that this peace is a shared peace that is freely granted to us because of Jesus Christ. Mankind has been reconciled back to God; Through justification by faith, we now have peace with God.

Trials come and they go. Oh, the peace that surpasses understanding is the peace that through it all, whatever state a Jesus Christ believer finds herself in, we have peace that surpasses understanding:

> *"Do not be anxious about anything, but in every situation, by prayer and petition, with thanksgiving, present your requests to God. And the peace of God, which transcends all understanding, will guard your hearts and your minds in Christ Jesus"* Philippians 4:7 (NIV).

Well. As much as I love Jesus, where was my peace when I could not handle a new day? There was a time when I could not pray, and did not want to pray. What was there to ask God other than bring back my son? *Please Lord, he had not accomplished what he wanted to yet. He was still very young. He never even settled down or married.*

The "peace of God" generally refers to a deep and abiding sense of tranquility and well-being that comes from having a close relationship with God, trusting in His promises, and surrendering one's worries and anxieties to Him in prayer. It is a peace that is not dependent on external circumstances but is rooted in faith and trust in God's sovereignty and goodness. Oh, did this become real to me when there were so many days, months, and what could have turned into years—where there was no tranquility. Where was the assurance found in Isaiah 26:3 (NIV) which says, "You will keep in perfect peace those whose minds are steadfast because they trust in you."

God has a way of showing us who He is and that His promises are true. Peace encompasses both inner peace deep down within, and peace in our relationships with others and with God. It is a fruit of the Holy Spirit, a result of faith in Jesus Christ, and a source of blessing for those who pursue it. God was guarding my heart and mind when I could not understand. After all, peace surpasses my capacity. That is the beauty of being kept in perfect peace. When things are imperfect and seemingly could not be any worse, there is still peace.

CHAPTER 19

Finding A New Normal

Dios usa cosas pequeñas para llamar tu atención.

"God uses small things to get your attention."

James and Hollie Coleman saved the day. They are high-spirited, good-natured blessings that God used to kickstart my healing and motivate me to find myself again. During the Spring of 2014, Hollie asked if I would like to take a Spanish class offered by her church. I welcomed her thoughtful invitation. A twelve-week course was on the path to healing, and recovery. It was a perfect reason get me out of the house and interact with people again. Not that I wasn't, but when you're going through the motions, you tend to miss out on a lot. I can't recall major events or personal milestones, but attending the Spanish class was a breath of fresh air.

One day a week, I learned Spanish with strangers who had no idea what I'd gone through. I made it a point not to miss the class even though I may have not wanted to go. The Colemans threw me a lifeline and I took it. The church members, who were mostly seniors, came in with excitement wanting to learn a new language. Every session we laughed and joked about our abilities. We roasted each other when one of us butchered the enunciation of Spanish words. None of the playful banter mattered. That Spanish class was a reminder that while I struggled to move on, there were others doing the same thing. They loved coming together and I loved seeing them all. It was okay that I didn't know anyone but James and Hollie. It didn't matter that everyone else never knew my name. As a matter of fact, I preferred it that way because it was one less empathetic look that I had to deal with.

Being with the group and learning Spanish was something I have always wanted to do. Learning Spanish required my full attention. That weekly meeting was revival to my soul. Something good was stirring and it was one that I wanted on repeat. When they say laughter is good for the soul, they are telling the truth! Each time a session ended, there were sweet afterthought chuckles about class that day. The class was like therapy without the credentials and God answered prayers was the result. I still can't speak Spanish and I can't even remember most of the words, but it was different. All I wanted was a reprieve and needed a moment to relax in the laughter.

By the time the sessions ended, I tried to find other avenues to keep myself engaged and busy. Thus, my pursuit to normalcy began. Embracing this new norm was odd. It seemed like a lifetime since this feeling came over me. There was this feeling of accomplishment and I wanted to pick up the phone to call Cameron but had to catch myself. That in itself angered me, and then I had to coach myself out of the mood. It still hurt like hell, but I became more determined each day to focus on getting better. Knowing that I still had to exist in this world for myself and those who were alive, I needed to start reinventing what normal would be. The class made me feel alive again. Laughing was the medicine I needed and that class was like filling a prescription. It was community. It was socializing. It required my commitment. And finally, it pulled on my brain to think and learn.

I don't know where you may be in your journey, but we all have to make it our priority to start somewhere. You can envision happiness all day, but if you never move towards it, it becomes nothing more than an unfulfilled dream. Traumatic experiences will alter directions and most if not all, fail to envision oneself as being whole, happy, and at peace. There are no manuals or how-to books that will prevent you from experiencing bad times. Most of them even fail to articulate your emotions and if we're honest they don't even come close to helping you conquer your despair. However, it can be done. This new feeling while taking Spanish gave me the fire to look for a repeat. I wanted to have those euphoric moments that pulled me out of despair. Preparing for class and being dedicated to something helped me to realize I am still alive and could still be lively. I wasn't concentrating on my problems 24/7. I wanted more.

DeMaris was in college during this time and needed my car to get to evening classes. Fridays were prayer at my church and I needed to be there. Prayer has always been my lifeline and if no one else was going to be in the sanctuary, Joycelyn Hall would be. To make things work, I decided to catch public transportation and walk the rest of the way to church. I would walk to the train station, get off a few towns later, and walk two miles to church. The commute was like taking steps in stride while listening to my favorite music from my iTunes playlist: Kirk Franklin, Kurt Carr, Myron Butler, Fred Hammond, Deitrick Haddon, and many more uplifting songs. Reflecting on just two of many changes brought the realization that I was experiencing emotional anchors. The quality of the events within community secured my safe space again.

Hearing positive music from the lyrics to the bass thumping changed my mood and kept me there until I turned it off. I would put those ear buds in and away I went to wherever I wanted to be. The therapy to my soul reflected progress with every step I took. I wasn't crying asking God to help, but rejoicing because He was still with me. I could sway, dance, and sing along to the lyrics which released tension in my body. Those walks were a chance to be attuned to the voice of God. What did He have to say? He seemed to be quiet while I was grieving, but He really wasn't. He was waiting for me to quiet down to hear. He waited for the panting to subside, and for ragged inhales and exhales. So, the music made me quiet. It was having a good workout and just reflecting on the sweat from the session. It made me reflect on the lyrics and breathe through the emotions to get me to a place of peace. Positive music was healthy for coping with the stress and boosted my psychological well-being.

I walked from August to October until it got too dark outside. Those walks were defining moments. They were sacred because I was pouring out my soul to God as I walked. My tears became my prayers. Crying out loud on the streets would have brought unwanted attention. I gave God everything that my heart could articulate—past failures, insecurities, disappointments, broken promises, and all the whys of my life. My conversation not only voiced the pain of losing my son, but it also became my plea for better. So, walking a couple of miles had purpose and was effective in helping me to recalibrate my emotions and feelings. By the time I got to church, I felt somewhat better as though some of the weight had dropped from my shoulders. My state of mind wasn't fixed overnight, but moving and getting out of the house was a start. You have to find that defining moment that will start you to move and identify what it will take to get you to another way of life. It's like having a deep cut that you recognize as painful and making moves to clean, disinfect, and cover the cut until its good enough for the cut to be exposed. It's not about getting full closure or even understanding your life-altering event. It's about doing something that will spark a fire in you. It is about nurturing the you that is still left. It's about shifting the emphasis from tragedy and pain to being free from its effects. Can you get back into life knowing that you still have a way to go to get you back to peace? It was worth a try.

I can see the path I'm on and what lies ahead. The road seems long, but the sun is shining.

It's not black anymore. The days are changing to hues of gray.

Being more determined to get back to a new normal, I spent time in prayer. All I wanted most was for God to help me to understand what happened and get me to a place where the loss was manageable. Searching out revelation from the Almighty meant I had no control. When you spend your adult life fixing, encouraging, normalizing other people's lives, you get a sense of self-accomplishment of being a fixer. However, I could not depend on those I "fixed" nor on myself because what exactly could I tell myself in a situation that I've never been in before?

There were too many on the sidelines looking and not speaking. Others checked in with occasional calls, but did not come over to lend their ear or shoulder. That's when I knew that if I was going to get back on track, I had to depend on God. I still believed. I still wanted my peace. So, who better than to birth it but God? I could have easily walked away, but I had the sense to know that God has always gotten me out of some sticky situations, healed me, provided, and cared. Drinking and doing drugs as an escape wasn't an option. I had to stick with what I knew, and ask the one who I knew had the answers.

One decision that I couldn't negotiate was living in an undesirable decision. Reflecting on the book of Job, the Bible gave me a relatable source for dealing with tragedy and survivor's suffering. Oftentimes we want to focus is on the end of the story where Job is restored, but no one wants to be able to endure an undesirable decision that cannot be overturned. Job lost his children and all of his livestock, mourns greatly and questions God. Why would such an event happen? God responds in a fashion that asks Job about his ability to counsel God, and whether Job perceived that his questions even recognized God's sovereignty and ability to make decisions. Job also has salt in his wound because of his wife who is bitter and tells Job to curse God and die. His friends? They question whether Job's life was sinful, as the cause of his own demise. Any one of us could insert ourselves into this scenario with grief. We can easily assume that God is punishing us due to our past mistakes. It could be taken a step further to even insert people who, unlike Job's friends, quietly critique our lives and come to conclusions that we did something wrong to deserve this pain. The answer is no. Regardless of your faith, truths, and denials, God's decision for death can ultimately release our loved ones from the pain they've endured. It also becomes our platform to show friends and strangers alike that we too go through difficult moments, but more importantly that we have great hope in believing that God's wisdom and compassion towards all far exceed our own desires. It is this truth as a Christian that I solely stood on with Cameron. There had to be a greater good no matter the state I was in.

Looking past myself was hard with all the statistics of murdered victims and the chance of bringing killers to justice. I had to believe in the sovereignty of God that justice would be served even though I may not see it in my lifetime should God decide. As difficult and painful that revelation was, I had to become more determined to capture my peace by knowing that my son would not have to endure cruelty, selfishness, and an evil world. God the Father wasn't trying to punish me through death; He was releasing Cameron by death to bring him home. It's thought-provoking, right? If we all could get past thinking that God wants to hurt us and focus upon His love for our loved ones that far exceeds our abilities to save them from evil or sickness, we would be at peace. Do we fare better than God? Would our selfishness in keeping them alive become selflessness in allowing them to obtain their own peace? Is it possible that Cameron's total peace relied on not living on this earth? No matter which way I sliced the truth, it was the truth that brought me and my family to this ordeal, and the truth would bring us through it.

It's been more than a year since Cameron's death when I started looking for avenues to shift my focus from being a grieving parent to a living parent with a loss. Every day was a new day with an affirmation to speak over what the day would look like. In January 2018, I was on Facebook and found a woman who spoke on framing your world with your words. That woman was the late Pastor Cassandra Elliott. For thirty days, she went on Facebook Live and provided the daily word and the supporting scriptures that began to shape my course back to peace. In these forty-five-minute teachings, she challenged the listeners to reverse all the negativity of speech and thought, and to look to positive language that would propel them onto the road of success.

Everything wasn't looking black.

It was still dark, but not as dark as the day before. I had a journal and pen with the hope of looking at life with expectation, hope, excitement, and peace. By the time it was over, I knew that God was answering my prayers. Though I was looking at people who I had known personally for years and those closest to me to fix my brokenness, it was a stranger who had a heart for speaking positive messages that moved me from black to light gray days. At the end of thirty days, Pastor Elliott offered a challenge called Bounce Back University. This twelve-week program would allow those who had challenges and setbacks the opportunity to release, recover and bounce back. At first, I wasn't sure I wanted to participate. Knowing that it would require me to be transparent, I wasn't sure that I wanted the wound to be cut open again. But, I signed up anyway and over the next few weeks, women who had every type of setback joined the group. Pastor Elliott's commitment to bringing closure to a lot of our issues sparked something in me.

Closure. That's what I desired most even though the murderer was still out there. Yet, I had to come to terms with the fact that my closure was not contingent upon a killer being caught. I could have closure in knowing that Cameron's life was full and that he was loved. As far as Cameron's life was concerned, I would get closure.

Bounce Back University helped me to strategize how to get out of the pit I was in. I did not have to continue to live under the shadow of grief. One of the private conversations with Pastor Elliott dealt with uncovering other hidden hurts that no one knew about. I guess you can say that the band-aid was ripped off again, but this time, it focused on all my issues, not just Cameron. When you begin to realize that transparency reveals the ugliest, you can begin to see that the root of your problem may not be the last painful situation, but the one that crosses the line in opening pandora's box. What God ultimately wanted from me was to give Him all of my pain from my young adult years until now. How could I be fully healed if I only gave God a portion of my pain? I had the opportunity to change. My way forward was through this community of women. I enjoyed participating in Bounce Back University. Just the words of wisdom alone brought back my appetite for life. When you've been emptied of a season, the hunger for more seems to be a faraway notion.

At the end of the sessions, I wanted more. Searching out new ways of positively filling my time was exciting. In the fall of 2018, Pastor Cassandra Elliott invited me to be one of the instructors. Beyond being honored, it gave me a sense of purpose and I was more determined than ever not to allow my situation to determine my future. That assignment pulled me out of gave me a reason to return to living and not merely existing. There were people out there who needed to see what a comeback looked like. If I failed, then folks would perceive that God failed, which He doesn't. What fails is our ability to control every situation and believe that no one cares. Moving from existing to living takes effort. Deciding to get out of bed, eat, shower and dress took energy and a desire for more. There is so much to lose in just existing. How can one maintain any relationship without working to get the best out of it? Nowhere in the Bible does God speak about existing.

From the beginning of time, God's breath brought life and His words brought a command to be fruitful and multiply. Though I was taken off course for a moment, I still had fruit. I still had a purpose to pursue and a promise to be fulfilled. My personal dreams and aspirations for myself didn't leave when Cameron died; They just needed to be pruned. They needed a push.

My days were becoming hues of gray…the newness of dawn is approaching.

CHAPTER 20

BREATHING AGAIN

I don't know the exact day, but I know that I gradually began living. Just like the day came where I almost lost my mind, the day came when I woke up and realized my heart was not hurting. The funny part of that return to peace instigated an inquiry. *Why was I having a good day?* That good day stretched out to days and then weeks and finally months. My path to peace was being able to get through the day without tears or without trying to reflect on what I lost. It took some time to get through these milestones, but I did.

I could never forget Cameron, but I could lessen that impact by remembering God's love and promise that He would be there in the midst of my troubles. If I had to look back from July 2013, I could attest that every battle won had its scars. My heart has the biggest cut, like chop suey-mangled, yet it was always in the Master's hands and still beating. Now that I had peace in my life, it took on its own identity making me accountable and reflective on a daily basis. Peace required that my daily routine be affirmative and not degrading moments. Some say that going through these traumatic experiences can make or break an individual. It does. What needs to be asked is how do you recover when you've been broken? That in itself is a major feat. In no way would I ever be able to forget my firstborn, but I had to come to a place where I had to move on. The harshest memories like the dreaded call had to be placed far in my memory banks. Every time they tried to rear a head, I visualized throwing it back in the box or taking paper and throwing it in a roaring fire. These acts over time moved me out of always thinking on the bad parts to controlling what thoughts I allowed to surface. I'm still broken, but peace is keeping me.

What have I gained from peace? It's become my anchor. Anchors on any vessel great or small can keep them from running onshore and keep them still in the water. If we see peace as the anchor of our lives, then we know that regardless of life it can provide stability. We can superficially look at people and think they have it all together without knowing if peace exists. The opportunity for peace to shine is when critical events that should in most eyes cause many to fall or give up, doesn't. That's when I understood the peace that I gained in my walk. I didn't do what most people expected. In fact, a lot was amazed at the calm I possessed though, during the first few years, I wasn't. My peace was activated in my prayer time, speaking to God about my heartache and him responding with his love. Knowing that he had the confidence in me to recover fully made me relax and be accepting of life. Acceptance of living beyond death has to be the main sustaining factor in the recovery process. Forcing to live in continual denial creates bondage. Not only are you denying the reality of your situation, but also the ability to live. No boxer is going to stay down after a TKO. They're going to accept their loss, recover from their wounds and try again. Getting to peace is trying again after the TKO. It's getting back up; it's understanding the impact and it's knowing that we all can continue to live after the loss. If anyone is at the point of not getting to this juncture, then I suggest therapy. Somehow, we must return back to being functional. The longer one stays in bondage, the harder it is for recovery to happen.

Peace was driving me to be accepting of all that happened. At no point did I give up on ever being back to myself again. I wanted to live and the determination that was settling moved me from the place of dark thinking into hoping. One of the many obstacles faced was my attitude toward life in general. Remember that grieving places you in a dark moment and it will contribute to the woe-is-me thinking. When I had enough of being in a state of depression and grief, my mindset had to be challenged. Looking at my adjusted life required me to seek out positive people, places, and events incorporating them into a daily routine. Seeking positive people meant keeping away from negative voices. I limited myself to friends that really had their own struggles. Why? Because it was a sign that they hadn't achieved securing peace in their lives. I sought out people whose idea of life aligned with what I was looking for and I asked for accountability in achieving those results. Pastor Elliott's Bounce Back group teamed us all with accountability partners. The goal was to keep the pulse on the steps taken to recover while forming relationships. Encouragement goes a long way even when you can't see your steps. These women created a new network and made me focus more on getting it right.

My recovery became my testimony. I never realized how many people were looking at me and how I walked through this. What they saw was the smile that rose from pain. There came a time when a co-worker lost a family member. The person came to me and just sat with tears. I knew at that moment that they came for comfort because they understood where I've been. God placed me in a position to minister and give them hope. When I see others who have gone through the same pain, I can't help but to empathize with them. God places people in our lives to give them the Word of God and to show His lovingkindness and tender mercies. I never thought that this pain would connect me with others who have had the same experience. But it does.

I recall connecting with a group of women for a mentoring project that my friend was hosting. As she began introducing each of the women on the phone call, most had the same shared experience—they had close family members who were victims of murder. This is not something that you ignore. One dealt with a gang-related shooting while another had a murder-suicide in her family. Next thing I knew, there I was sharing my story. Once you start to put things into perspective, no one is excluded. There isn't a single people group that isn't impacted by death. Though it would seem that based on location and status that somehow it would be different for some, but no, it's not. This seems like common sense, but that thought leaves quickly when you're placed in a predicament that you didn't see coming. Yeah, I could relate to this group. We didn't all come from the same background, yet these women had the same response as me. As we continued the discussion, I could see the pain and resilience of moving forward and other women walking out their peace. It was another outlet for me to express and be safe in doing so. These new sisters became my source of strength as I became theirs. Just knowing that there was a genuine spirit between us made releasing easier. It was an opportunity to stretch myself in sharing, but more importantly, the genuine exchange showed them that they could return to peace, too. Yes, it defined my next season, purpose and perspective. I knew this was what I was called to do, to be that flashlight, hand, shoulder, ear or anything that they needed me to be. I survived, broken but blessed.

CHAPTER 21

LESSON

As I reflect back in the 10th year of being without my son, I realize that if I didn't know God in a relational sense, I would still be struggling to try to come to grips with his death. When my best friend lost her mother back in 2007, it impacted her world. She had lived with her mother all her life and at the age of fifty, she struggled with moving forward without her mom. Amongst dealing with grief, my friend had to try and live a life that solely depended on her. She had to make a lot of decisions that, in most cases, her mother usually made. My friend's income spiraled down quickly because she wasn't working due to an injury and her mother had shared the living expenses. I felt helpless because I had no idea of how to even begin to motivate and inspire her to keep living. My friend become a shell of a person who just existed as the days passed. So, when death entered my life, I was determined not to become what I saw my friend as a hopeless existence. I had too much to live for and knowing that all of this that I was going through had a purpose. I kept asking the Lord why I and he kept showing me that my way back to living in peace had a bigger meaning. He was able to show me that there were people who were suffering from this and needed someone who had the compassion to listen and be that support they needed.

As much as I wanted this not to be my life, it is what God revealed to me. I didn't realize that people were watching how I reacted after my son passed away. Friends and co-workers from time to time would come to me and say, "I don't know how you did it," and I would look at them confused for not understanding their comments.

However, what they really meant was *how can you be so at peace with all that you've gone through?* My response was truthful and to the point: God. If there's one piece of advice that I could give to those who just couldn't recover from loss is to know that God loved our beloved as much as He loves us. My son had a prayer that God heard. Truthfully speaking, our loved ones may have prayed for God to give them relief from the agony that they were going through. We shouldn't convince ourselves that we have a greater prayer than one who is prays for themselves. When I think about Cameron, I often wonder if he really wanted to leave this earth. Maybe the pain and disappointment that he was going through was too much and even though he loved his family, he just wanted a way out. It's a tough pill to swallow, but God is wiser than we'll ever be. He loved Cameron and the sovereignty of God takes no counsel from the earth. Before life even began for Cameron, God knew his life expectancy. God gave our family the privilege of doing life with him for 26 years. If it were up to me, he'd still be alive. Some things do not pan out according to our plans. What I've come to learn is God knows best. So He gave us a surprise right before Cameron passed away.

CHAPTER 22

THE CHILDREN

Ahnya's Story – Little People

In 2012, I was blessed to see my angel for the first time. Her name is Ahnya and she's Cameron's daughter. Until 2012, we didn't know she existed, but Cameron received a call from her mother that she was his. When I laid my eyes on her, it was like looking at Cameron all over again. From the caramel skin to the almond-shaped eyes, Ahnya made life smile even brighter. I went to Atlanta to see her and spent a beautiful weekend celebrating her birthday. We went to the aquarium and the Coca-Cola museum. It was not long before Camron found out he was a father, and the tragedy of his death occurred. Ahnya was not exempted from this harsh reality.

By the time Cameron passed, Ahnya was six years old living in South Carolina with her aunt. I figured it would be best not to bring her to the services because I wanted to spare her from the pain as much as possible. Plus, mentally I wasn't in the frame of mind to even see her. My son's daughter has to continue living the rest of her life without her daddy. I hurt even more for her because she had just found out that he even existed. At the time that we met, she was only five years old. The unfairness of it all became too much to bear. I kept in close contact with her aunt and it killed me to know that she was suffering from all of this.

Even though we all were dealing with this nightmare, Ahnya was a gift. I had Cameron's legacy to consider. God blessed me with this small package and it was my responsibility to fulfill what Cameron couldn't. In the months that passed, I also found out that the young man that was claiming her as his died, too. If I thought that I had grief and pain, this little girl at the age of six was getting it even worse. How? How could this precious child lose both fathers in a matter of three months? Why was this even something I had to witness?

Ahnya taught me a few things about living. For one, she had a resilience to overcome. In looking at her position I did notice that she was devoid of emotions. She kept most at arm's length though she was looking for comfort. I knew that this was her defense mechanism trying to navigate through the pain she was experiencing. Her moments of rebellion had her crying out, not knowing how to express herself and we all had to respond with understanding and patience. As I began to spend time with her, she clearly had attributes of her father. It's amazing how children can emulate parents that they spend little time with. Her imagination kept me laughing as she took to my iPad creating video clips of her talking to her dolls. That was her escape and her peace. We became each other's support. She looked for understanding and comfort and I looked for my son's legacy through the rambunctious eyes of a little angel. Ahnya spent just a few moments in her life loving her father, yet she kept going. She didn't dwell in the past. No. She pushed herself to embrace her today and looked forward to another day.

Don't forget the children. Children who go through loss are no different than you or me. They need our assurance that they will get through this pain, but they can also bring us such joy if we can see past our own pain. Ahnya had her bad days, acting out in school and at home. I just had to be sensitive to what was going on. We can't attribute a child's demeanor to them just being rebellious. Look at what has been presented before them. If I'm struggling with dealing with death, then I couldn't disregard Ahnya's struggle for the same thing.

Even though my son, DeMaris, was nineteen when his brother died, he was still a young adult. I paid close attention to how he was dealing with grief. His jovial personality that everyone was used to seeing had been tinged with sadness. He was quiet. He had no desire to do anything. What I did notice is that he took on the characteristics of Cameron. It was eerie and amazing to see the transformation. DeMaris decided to loc his hair and grow a full beard. His laugh mirrors the tone and pitch of Cameron. One night I heard him laughing and nearly came unglued because it sounded so much like Cameron. When I said something to DeMaris, he just shrugged his shoulders. The endearment "Miss Lady" was Cameron's calling card. When we talked on the phone or chat via messenger, that would be used. DeMaris didn't skip a beat in addressing me with this endearment and hasn't stopped.

DeMaris did get into some trouble and he went to counseling. He had been to court multiple times for driving offenses and I could see what this was about to turn into. In one court appearance, the judge ordered counseling. I started looking for additional counseling through mentoring programs and any adult man willing to take time with him. One thing I was determined to do was to make sure that his path didn't mirror his brother's.

Young adults going through this difficult process have more avenues of getting into trouble. Drugs, alcohol, and promiscuity are just the tip of the iceberg and it should be the family as a whole that needs to ensure no child is left behind in returning to a place of peace. Take them with you as you get yourself back to living again.

If they need to go to counseling, put pride away and get them the help they need. Don't assume their quietness as their acceptance of death or any earth-shattering event. Give them an environment that will allow them to express themselves without criticism or rebuke. I did this for my only son. I never stopped talking to him, asking about his day or how he was feeling. I spent time creating new memories with him and giving him space when he needed it.

I got away from arguing when he wasn't doing as expected and changed the strategy of explaining the repercussions of his actions. If we are going to save our children, get them the help they deserve.

CHAPTER 23

Forgiveness

Honestly, not knowing who did this to Cameron still bothers me. Although I have forgiven the killer doesn't mean I don't want justice. My prayers have been for those involved to be caught and tried. We need strong, fail-proof evidence to put them away for life. A crime was committed against my son and I want justice to prevail. Ten years later, and his murder case is now a cold case. No leads, no arrests, not a word. My son is part of a growing statistic of unsolved murders. Even though there has been no recent developments in his case, prayerfully the Georgia Bureau of Investigation will never stop looking for the killer. The more I see the news, the more I pray for justice to be swift.

Too many unsolved murders and too many silent voices have kept Cameron and many others from receiving their true rest. We need to remove this "silent code" of allowing criminals escape routes and ensure that families who are suffering get the response they need to close the door and bring some sort of resolution. Justice starts at home and we need to train our children to tell when something isn't right. Our news feeds, social media, and all sorts of communique are full of violence that society seems to treat as a sporting event. We have lost our abilities to diffuse anger and respond with reasoning.

Society no longer has social skills and our children have been taught through these outlets to become relentless in getting more likes than to build and foster lasting relationships.

Unforgiveness can prolong you from recovering and I learned this quickly when leveling my emotions as a grieving mother. It's so easy to become bitter and distance ourselves from people we believe have offended us. More importantly, we harbor those feelings and transfer this to other areas of our lives.

First, learn to forgive yourself.

I had to do it for myself because as a mother I felt that I let my son down and this was the reason why he was in this predicament. As a parent, we want what's best for our children. We will move heaven and earth to make sure that our children have everything we think we were denied. A part of my struggle was to come to grips that though my son was 26 years old, he was accountable for himself. I did all that a mother could and knew that I provided him a sound foundation that could be used for success.

Second, forgive the deceased. Yes, I had to forgive Cameron. I was so angry and hurt that I resented that he didn't come home before his death. Even more so, that he died so young. I was constantly reflecting upon what I lost in his death that I grew to resent. Though it's not mentioned, we do have those feelings, and it's never dealt with because any conversations leaning towards those feelings are either ignored or treated poorly. Letting go of these emotions and really addressing them will help to foster peace. We don't know why death comes early to the young or the ones we love dearly – it's a God thing. Trying to rationalize the whys only frustrates you more and keeps you bound longer than you need to be. It's hard to release and forgive when the individual is not around to receive. Pray and ask the Father to help you to release the pain and forgive. I think of Cameron's life as one that was complete even though it was early. I know that based on all that he went through, his place with Christ is far more rewarding than suffering on this earth.

Third, forgive those who failed to step up to the plate. Those who have failed to show up in any capacity when you felt you needed the help, release them from your expectations. Here's what helped me: they weren't qualified. Realize that people may not have the capacity to assist in your needs. Only God can. You have people who panic when bad news comes. Then there are others who hate going to viewings, funerals, or memorials. You'll also find people who believe that you're okay because you haven't said anything and know you're grieving. However, embrace those who answered the call and were there for you.

God has the ability to give you what you need when it's needed the most. I found that to be true when those members in the body of Christ began to come. They were individuals that I didn't even know who knew me. These are the people who I cherished the most during my darkest days. I'm grateful that they had a heart for God's people and made themselves available to assist. Turn your negatives into positives and begin to move past those who didn't show up.

Finally, and most importantly, God. Are you still mad at God for not saving your loved one? Do you blame Him for the pain and depression that won't seem to break? If you're in this position, I understand. When I began to realize that God loved me and my son, I knew that the decision of life and death I had no control over. God loved Cameron enough to release him from this life to be with Him in another. God has compassion for His creation, and when they cry out, He answers. Though we believe that the prayers we pray are in alignment with others, at times that's not the case. *God's will be done on earth as it is in Heaven*, which takes on a new meaning when we come to the understanding we want to be in agreement with God's decisions. God the Father is compassionate and loving. No parent wants to see their children crying or suffering and they will do whatever is necessary to change the outcome.

Does God care for us all? Yes, He does. My son was loved by God and I know that his prayers were for a better life—one where he could be free from pain and disappointment. I wanted that also for Cameron and his departure left us in pain and without answers. I have to believe that God took him from this unforgiving earth to rejoice and shout eternally in Heaven. That's why I'm able to release, forgive and be at peace. God hasn't left you hopeless nor has he abandoned you. It's the opposite. He has given you an answer that you weren't expecting. When I think about the prayers for my son just days before his death and the intensity, I realize that God was responding.

Death isn't the end as it's a transition. Everything we do from the initial impact until now, we are adjusting our lives to counterbalance death.

The Bible teaches us that Holy Spirit will comfort and give snippets of revelation to show that the Father's decision is perfect. The sufferings of this world are not even worthy comparison to when God's children reach Heaven! If you're a mother – do you even remember the actual pains of labor? Can you recall the pains of surgery, a toothache, or broken bones? You may be able to describe the pain, but to relive it cannot be done. So, begin to thank God that your loved one's suffering is not even a thought while they're rejoicing in Heaven. Hallelujah!

CHAPTER 24

I AM A WITNESS

I can truly say I have learned a lot about myself during this journey. I know that every covered issue that I had, came to the surface. One major issue was fear. Cameron's death brought out the worst when it came to my family. I would have minor panic attacks if I couldn't reach any of them on the phone. The paranoia of thinking the worst overtook my logic and created all of these fictitious scenarios in my head. The test came when DeMaris decided that he wanted to move to Georgia. He wanted a new start so I spoke to his uncle who agreed Demaris could stay with him. I tried my best to persuade him not to leave. The thought of him being in the same state that Cameron had died in was enough to send me to an asylum. I don't think DeMaris even knew the heightened fear that came upon me knowing that he was walking in the same steps as his brother. How could I even explain to DeMaris my fears? Plus, the way I even found out—two weeks before he was leaving—was unnerving.

While arguing with DeMaris, my brother Joe found an apartment and was moving out by the end of the month. He told me days before leaving also. All of this occurring in the same week was a punch in my gut. With my fears at an ultimate high, I began to believe that I would not be able to survive being alone in the house. At the end of March 2016, DeMaris boarded a plane heading for Georgia and by the end of the same week, Joe had moved out. Now, I had to deal with abandonment issues. I couldn't understand why God would punish me again by having this happen with both of them being my support. I cried for a week behind these moves. It got so bad that I think I was afraid of my own shadow. I had been living in my own house for ten years, so I knew every creak in the house yet without DeMaris and Joe I felt like I was in a different house. I wholeheartedly felt as though both my brother and son abandoned me to pursue life.

I wanted the same for myself but was still struggling. Why now? Could they not have stayed longer? I know now that God wanted me to deal with my fears of being by myself. Three years passed and though nothing was resolved with the case, I was forced to continue moving. The rug had been pulled from underneath me for a second, making no sense and seemingly unfair. I spent days crying trying to rationalize why. Once I got over crying, I started taking a look around my house and doing some cleaning– ridding myself of the clutter that was packed in corners.

Since 2013, I'm not sure I did anything to the house. Coming and going was autopilot in my life and just doing the minimum only created a collection of stuff that I had no idea even existed. Once I had to live alone, it became apparent that my focus needed to change. In taking an assessment of my life, seeing the clutter brought me to the realization that I had not been living. Though I existed because I wanted to, I didn't live. My house was the replica of what I was doing—nothing. I spent my weekends purging and solicited help from my friend, Everett, who answered my plea and lifted heavy things that needed to be put out.

Some of the items I purged belonged to Cameron. It was hard releasing them, as if tossing out his things meant I was tossing him out. I didn't want him to leave and me holding onto all of his things was my answer to keeping him alive. As I looked through papers, it was reminiscent of going through his life and made me smile at his many accomplishments. He had artwork, school and music compositions, clothes, and many pictures. However, like with anything, I had to decide what to keep and what to throw out. It was a struggle, but I got through it. It's amazing how being traumatized makes discarding a piece of paper a daunting task. You never know how difficult looking at childhood memories and the stories behind them make it a tough decision to place them in a recycle bag. It's like ripping open an old wound, but it is necessary. To be able to move again and be at a place where you can accept the outcome, there has to be a purging that will relieve and heal at the same time. Moving doesn't mean forgetting. It's not a criminal act or amoral to make decisions to close certain chapters in our lives. With this purging that I did in my house, I kept the best of Cameron. He had made tables during his wood carving class in school. They were sound and sturdy, full of skill and potential. I also kept his artwork, full of promise and mastery. His compositions are a gem, full of compassion and life. Cameron left this family with much life and love that will be longstanding. It's okay to get rid of the clutter.

I started to settle into a routine of finding little things to do and realizing how peace was overtaking my life. Feeling abandoned evolved into enjoying being by myself. The fear of not having my family in my house was reduced greatly, but I still had my concerns for DeMaris. I made sure that we talked often, and I would drop subtle hints about staying away from Atlanta, though it didn't work. My brother only lived minutes from me and I didn't have to consider others in my house nor did I have to come home directly after work. I had space and opportunity to do anything I wanted. Spending quality time with myself and doing things outside of the norm felt really good. I began to pray more at home. Not that I didn't pray, but because I had no one in the house, I could pray as loud and long as I wanted and not disturb a soul. After about two months, I enjoyed my freedom and came home to what I recreated. My home became a peaceful place where my fears were no longer a threat. The fears of DeMaris being hurt in Georgia were gone. God had begun to show me that trusting in Him created the benefits that I needed to keep moving on the pathway of peace and recovery. That was a big milestone in knowing that I could keep moving forward – not looking back at where I was but where I could be at the end of this journey.

There's a break in this dark cloud that has been over my head.

I can see the path before me, dimly lit but it's there.

A voice whispers to me, compelling me to take the step.

I don't seem to care where I've been.

Why? Because light is near.

Every day is a different story and emotion. One minute you're smiling and a minute later crying. The rollercoaster for me lasted for months with a variety of triggers. A sunny day would have me crying, especially seeing clouds because I associated them with heaven. I would be crying while driving, praying that I wouldn't run into the back of another car. On the other hand, watching the Philadelphia Eagles play always makes me smile because Cameron was an avid fan. When they won the Super Bowl in 2018, I felt like he was with me even though it was a bitter-sweet moment of us not sharing this monumental moment. Experiencing triggers regardless of the tragic event can alter anyone of us daily, but managing them will determine your outcome. Oftentimes I felt off guard looking for an escape that would afford me time to get my emotions together. How do you explain to someone that you had a trigger? Most times you don't. Unless your circle or associations have experienced some level of trauma, they will not understand the psychological mechanisms that respond to the emotional threat. Falling apart was not my intention, so I did whatever it took not to let anyone see me cry. Yet, in the same breath, I was tired of acting the part while trying to figure it out. One major ah-ha was accepting that I didn't have to hide my pain.

When you are portrayed as being strong, people assume that you aren't affected by your pain or that your recovery from the event has somehow put you back on track. That is farthest from the truth. Strong people are the most wounded and can't articulate the pain because in their eyes such emotion would be deemed a sign of weakness. Better yet, how do you cry without cussing or screaming without looking crazy? I had to understand that it was okay to be weak. Didn't I just experience a tragic event? The other struggle was wondering what people would say if I broke down. That too was something I had to abandon. I was subjecting myself to a lot of medical and emotional issues by suppressing my pain.

Therefore, I allowed myself to cry or become agitated when these occurrences happened. I learned quickly to shut down emotional threats by voicing my triggers. After Cameron, you can't get me to watch anything dealing with murder. I avoid movies, social media, and news to spare myself from recurring trauma. I know that I can't avoid everything, but I at least convey my position to my friends and family. I have to matter. My peace has to take precedence over everything. When I came back to myself, my peace had to be in every part of my moving forward. When you're living within the confines of peace, you guard it. I don't allow people to shift me out of what I have strived to obtain. People may never understand your actions, but you become okay to exist in whatever makes you okay. When I look back at the journey, there is no way that I would subject myself to events that make me want to lose it. Peace is daily for me. Peace keeps me focused. Peace allows me to cry even after nine years and soothes me when I need comforting. My pathway invited strangers who made me laugh, celebrated my success, and cried with me when I was at my most vulnerable.

Every day is a decision that you have to do something different. Everyone's road to obtain peace is different, but it's shared by those who have gone through it. I have heard many times and am a firm believer that we all can make it through dark times. We just need to learn to manage life in a way that we are not consumed by grief but live restored. I can't tell you when life will become lighter, but I can attest that it will. Be determined to live life knowing that your loved one is no longer suffering in this unsettling world. My life management is praying and believing for those who, like me, are in a place of helplessness and can see the light on their pathway. I see myself as a puller since I've been there. I reach and pull anyone with the faith and belief that they, too, will return to peace.

During my journey, a woman in North Carolina whose son died from a stray bullet reached out to me. Like me, she had no leads or answers to who murdered her son, only the pain of it all. As I began to talk, I identified with exactly where she was emotionally and allowed her to express herself freely. That's what she needed. Someone who could understand the pain and position of death. People are looking for us. They are looking for those who have gone through similar life-changing situations. Even though no one goes through the exact experience of another, it helps to know that others have been through something similar. In the end, those who endure tragedy want to be at a place of peace. When I told God that I trusted Him, I never imagined that I would be a shoulder for someone, or an ear just to listen to the pain. People don't want to be judged for the expression of their pain, they want ears and hearts that will help them get through the season to beat this and become functional again. This world is looking for success stories of overcomers and those who dare to fight.

In August of 2019, I received a call from one of my dearest friends. Her son had passed away from an undetected illness. I was stunned into silence and pulled the car over because there was such a sense of helplessness. She told me that she, and her husband, had just left the funeral home and asked that my brother and I be a part of the services. The pain I heard in her voice as she cried was all too familiar. The overwhelming sense of "why me" and "how do I live" was unconsciously spoken. Yet, she called me for help and I had to respond by showing up at her doorstep. I had to become what I needed—a relatable friend. As much strength as I could possibly give her, we took a walk. I walked with her sharing my testimony and what she would be experiencing. My brother Joe spoke to her husband. Once I left, I prayed that maybe one comment I made did the difference for her. When I say this is not something you would wish on your friends or enemies, it's the truth. When I looked into her eyes and heard the strain in her voice, I knew. I don't care how many times you hear about someone passing, it brings back that sting to the heart.

By November, I decided to call her. I've been keeping up with her just to see where she is emotionally. Everything she's feeling I have felt. I allow her to talk because she needs that outlet and she knows I know how she's feeling as a mother. She told me, "That walk we took did something for me. You don't know how much I needed that." I want to believe that my return to peace was the difference. God knows what it took. If we can go from faith to faith and glory to glory, my testimony is that I have gone from peace to peace. My hope is to be able to hold onto her so that she will get there. I also want to believe that the walk itself was a symbol of me holding her hand and putting her, and all those who need it, on the pathway to obtain peace. We don't have to live without it.

So then, the question becomes, "Who are you amid adversity?" As a child of God, people are looking for signs of weakness. When I reflect on the book of Job in the Bible, his friends thought he had done something wrong. They were curious as to why Job was subjected to such pain after the death of his family. Job's wife thought it best to curse God and die.

Sometimes we believe that our pain is based on God's punishment and not the reality of life. Aren't we all in this world together? God said that the wheat and tares would grow together. We as children serving God are subject to all things on the earth. Health issues, sunshine, rain, and all four seasons are what we who are on the earth will endure. My son's death had me in the spotlight, not because of the incident itself but it was a birthing of testimony and a ministry designed to help those who have experienced the same pain. Some people were astonished at how well I recovered. As they began to ask questions, I was able to give them my testimony of how good God is. Even during my recovery, I had co-workers who lost parents, and through understanding of their pain, I was enlisted to pray and give comfort.

I am who I am because of the design of the Father. I have chosen to live because I wanted to tell my story to someone who was struggling with life. Others can live a life of peace and be able to navigate through life knowing that the love of the Father towards them exists. The peace that has been forfeited can be obtained. Through Jesus Christ, there is peace. This is the life that I chose to live years before Cameron's death. I always wanted to help people but no way could I have ever imagined that it took something like this tragedy to evolve to this. The peace that I now have makes me see what most cannot. My empathy for those who have suffered loss creates the atmosphere for people to come and talk. I'm convinced that people just need the ear and the compassion to help them see through their pain.

Now I manage my life with a keen awareness that at any moment, it can be altered. It has nothing to do with being scared or having some levels of anxiety. It has more to do with making sure that you experience life in its fullness. You can spend the rest of your life regretting decisions or you can accept that you made poor decisions, learned from them, and continued forward.

That is living in peace. My pathway brought me to a place of acceptance of Cameron's decision, of God's love, and my future. I will never admit to having all the answers, but I can attest that it took trial and error to get me to the place of peace. The sovereignty of God does not need counsel from us. God's plan for each of us is not predicated on another's ability or inability to serve. God desires that we grow in Him and become servants of the Kingdom of God.

The path of my peace is as bright as the noon-day sun. The Light in my life gives me a wave of peace like no other. As I look behind to see the path to my victory, the storm I left behind is overshadowed by peace.

Made in the USA
Middletown, DE
10 April 2024